# MUST-KNOW
# FRENCH

# MUST-KNOW FRENCH

## 4,000 Words That Give You the Power to Communicate

Eliane Kurbegov

Illustrations by Jason Fennell

**McGraw·Hill**

New York   Chicago   San Francisco   Lisbon   London   Madrid   Mexico City
Milan   New Delhi   San Juan   Seoul   Singapore   Sydney   Toronto

1 2 3 4 5 6 7 8 9 0 FGR/FGR 0 9 8 7 6


ISBN-13: 978-0-07-145644-9
ISBN-10:    0-07-145644-9
Library of Congress Control Number: 2006920586

Interior design by Blue Mammoth Design
Interior illustrations by Jason Fennell

McGraw-Hill books are available at special quantity discounts to use as premiums and sales promotions, or for use in corporate training programs. For more information, please write to the Director of Special Sales, Professional Publishing, McGraw-Hill, Two Penn Plaza, New York, NY 10121-2298. Or contact your local bookstore.

This book is printed on acid-free paper.

# Contents

## 3 The Human Body, Health, and Medicine

## 6 A Place to Live

## 7 At Work

## 10   Society and Government

## 11   Nature and the Environment

## 12   Measures, Numbers, and Time

# Introduction

Congratulations! You've decided to study French! And now you want to be able to find all the right words for a specific topic in one place. *Must-Know French* is what you need. This book can be useful at any level of learning. It will reinforce what you already know and help you broaden your vocabulary by building on prior knowledge.

*Must-Know French* exposes you to current terminology in the French language. As the world changes around you, so does language. With technological progress and globalization, new language is created at such a rapid pace that dictionaries and traditional books are challenged to respond appropriately. In the world of business, travel, and academics, or simply in daily life, the power to communicate in French is a valuable skill. Precise vocabulary is a key element to convey and understand clear messages. Four thousand basic and more advanced terms were carefully selected and grouped by subject matter in twelve units throughout this book. Knowing these terms will enable you to communicate more easily in all kinds of situations.

Lexical terms are grouped thematically (education, shopping, travel, etc.). First you will identify cognates and familiar words like *le téléphone* or *la loterie*; then you can focus on new vocabulary. However, new words and unfamiliar expressions will be easy to grasp and remember because they belong to a common semantic field (i.e. *la fête*, *l'anniversaire*), or to a family of words (i.e. *la politique*, *le politicien*). Making these connections alleviates the memorization effort. To further facilitate instant recall, idiomatic expressions such as "*Il fait froid*" are presented as vocabulary items where vocabulary and structure are intertwined.

*Must-Know French* contains twelve thematic vocabulary units such as Communication, Health, Leisure, Work, and other important topics. Each unit is further subdivided into content-based clusters to make it easy for self-learners to find vocabulary pertaining to individual needs. *Must-Know French* includes useful and common phrases to facilitate vocabulary acquisition in specific contexts. You will be able to recall and memorize these terms in meaningful situations.

A typical page consists of words or phrases translated from English to French. For easier and faster access to terms, the listings are presented in alphabetical order whenever possible and omit the preposition *to* before infinitive verbs. Within the listings, the definite article is omitted for English nouns but included for French nouns to alert readers to their gender.

Numerous sentences are offered in both English and French to help highlight or clarify the meaning and usage of various terms. The Must-Know Tips, located throughout each section, will alert readers to linguistic devices such as idiomatic expressions, false cognates, and structures that may be problematic to the English speaker.

Most importantly, over 100 interesting and fun exercises supplement the content-based units. Some exercises are based on recognition skills such as finding the intruder in a series of terms, or identifying the correct meaning of a phrase. Others are more challenging contextualized activities. For example, you will reconstruct the chronological order in a sequence of events, match a question with its answer, and reconstitute a dialogue between a salesperson and a client. The numerous exercises, accompanied by the answer key at the back of the book, give you the choice of undertaking simple or more difficult tasks, and help you assess both your existing knowledge and your progress. Just like the vocabulary units, each of the exercises has a theme. Pick and choose as you will!

Learning and mastering other languages is sometimes challenging yet always rewarding. You will find *Must-Know French* indispensable and invaluable in your quest to expand your communication skills in French.

# MUST-KNOW
# FRENCH

# 1

# *Communicating with Others*

# Introductions, Greetings, and Farewells

## Personal Information | ## Renseignements personnels

| | |
|---|---|
| address (electronic) | l'adresse (électronique) (f) |
| age | l'âge (m) |
| city/town | la ville |
| divorced | divorcé(e) |
| engaged | fiancé(e) |
| first name | le prénom |
| last name | le nom de famille |
| married | marié(e) |
| neighborhood | le quartier |
| *In what neighborhood do you live?* | *Dans quel quartier habitez-vous?* |
| occupation | l'occupation (f) |
| separated | séparé(e) |
| single | célibataire |
| telephone number | le numéro de téléphone |
| *Here is my cell phone number.* | *Voici mon numéro de portable.* |
| widowed | veuf(-ve) |

## Greetings and Farewells | ## Salutations

| | |
|---|---|
| answer | répondre |
| call | téléphoner |
| delighted | enchanté(e) |
| don't mention it | il n'y a pas de quoi |
| good-bye | au revoir |
| hello | bonjour/allô |
| *Hello. I am listening.* | *Allô. J'écoute.* |
| *Hope to see you again.* | *Au plaisir de vous revoir.* |
| *How are you?* | *Comment allez-vous?* |
| introduce (each other) | (se) présenter |
| leave a message | laisser un message |
| madam | madame |
| make a date/an appointment | prendre rendez-vous |

| meet | **rencontrer** |
| Madam/Mrs. | **Madame/Mme** |
| Miss | **Mademoiselle/Mlle** |
| Mister/Sir/Mr. | **Monsieur/M.** |

 **Must-Know Tip**

Remember to use a title only in formal settings: ***Bonjour, monsieur/madame***.

In familiar settings use a title with a person's last name: ***Bonjour, Madame Leclerc***.

| *Remain on the line.* | *Ne quittez pas./Veuillez patienter.* |
| see you soon | **à bientôt** |
| thank you | **merci** |
| *Who's calling?* | *Qui est à l'appareil?* |
| *You are welcome.* | *Je vous en prie./De rien.* |
| wrong number | **le mauvais numéro** |
| *Sorry, you have the wrong number.* | *Désolé(e), vous avez le mauvais numéro.* |

# Parts of Speech

## Articles                     Les articles

**DEFINITE ARTICLES**

| the boy | **le garçon** |
| the girl | **la fille** |
| the man | **l'homme (m)** |
| the ladies | **les dames** |

**LES ARTICLES DÉFINIS**

**INDEFINITE ARTICLES**

| an apartment | **un appartement** |
| a house | **une maison** |
| some men | **des hommes** |

**LES ARTICLES INDÉFINIS**

## DEMONSTRATIVE ADJECTIVES

this book
this hotel
this picture
these people

## LES ADJECTIFS DÉMONSTRATIFS

**ce livre**
**cet hôtel**
**cette image**
**ces gens**

 **Must-Know Tip**

Remember to use the article **cet** instead of **ce** before a masculine singular noun starting with a vowel sound.

## POSSESSIVE ADJECTIVES

my father
my mother
my parents
your dog
your lady friend

## LES ADJECTIFS POSSESSIFS

**mon père**
**ma mère**
**mes parents**
**ton chien**
**ton amie**

 **Must-Know Tip**

Remember to use the possessive articles **mon, ton, son** instead of **ma, ta, sa** before a feminine singular noun starting with a vowel sound.

your bicycle
your friends
her fiancé
his wife
his/her children
*Her/His train leaves at seven o'clock.*
our trip
our clothes
your job

**ta bicyclette**
**tes amis**
**son fiancé**
**sa femme**
**ses enfants**
***Son train part à sept heures.***
**notre voyage**
**nos vêtements**
**votre emploi**

| | |
|---|---|
| your teachers | **vos professeurs** |
| their university | **leur université** |
| their classes | **leurs cours** |
| *Their friends are great!* | *Leurs amis sont super!* |

## Personal Pronouns

## Les pronoms personnels

| **SUBJECT PRONOUNS** | **LES PRONOMS SUJETS** |
|---|---|
| I | **je (j')** |
| you (sing.; familiar) | **tu** |
| he | **il** |
| she | **elle** |
| we | **nous** |
| you (pl.; formal) | **vous** |
| they | **ils/elles** |
| *Hi Guy! How are you?* | *Salut Guy! Comment vas-tu?* |
| *Hello madam. How are you?* | *Bonjour, madame. Comment allez-vous?* |

 **Must-Know Tip**

The impersonal subject pronoun **on** is used to express *we*, *one*, or *people*.

| **DIRECT OBJECT PRONOUNS** | **LES PRONOMS OBJETS DIRECTS** |
|---|---|
| him/it | **le** |
| her/it | **la** |
| them | **les** |
| *My parents? I love them.* | *Mes parents? Je les adore.* |

| **DIRECT/INDIRECT OBJECT PRONOUNS** | **LES PRONOMS OBJETS DIRECTS/INDIRECTS** |
|---|---|
| (to) me | **me** |
| (to) you (sing.; familiar) | **te** |
| (to) us | **nous** |

| | |
|---|---|
| (to) you (pl.; formal) | **vous** |
| *The policeman gives me a ticket.* | *Le gendarme me donne une contravention.* |
| *Give me your number!* | *Donne-moi ton numéro!* |

 **Must-Know Tip**

Remember that object pronouns are placed before the verb except in affirmative commands. Also remember to change the object pronouns **me** and **te** to **moi** and **toi** when placed after the verb in affirmative commands.

| | |
|---|---|
| **INDIRECT OBJECT PRONOUNS** | **LES PRONOMS OBJETS INDIRECTS** |
| to (for) him/to (for) her | **lui** |
| to (for) them | **leur** |
| *My friends? I speak to them every day.* | *Mes amis? Je leur parle tous les jours.* |

## Other Pronouns | ## Autres pronoms

| | |
|---|---|
| **POSSESSIVE PRONOUNS** | **PRONOMS POSSESSIFS** |
| mine | **le mien/la mienne/les miens/les miennes** |
| yours (sing.; familiar) | **le tien/la tienne/les tiens/les tiennes** |
| his/hers | **le sien/la sienne/les siens/les siennes** |
| *My courses are hard; hers are easy.* | *Mes cours sont difficiles; les siens sont faciles.* |
| ours | **le nôtre/la nôtre/les nôtres** |
| yours (pl.; formal) | **le vôtre/la vôtre/les vôtres** |
| theirs | **le leur/la leur/les leurs** |
| **DEMONSTRATIVE PRONOUNS** | **LES PRONOMS DÉMONSTRATIFS** |
| this one | **celui-ci/celle-ci** |

| | |
|---|---|
| *Both sweaters are pretty but this one is cheaper.* | *Les deux pulls sont jolis, mais celui-ci est moins cher.* |
| that one | **celui-là/celle-là** |
| these | **ceux-ci/celles-ci** |
| those | **ceux-là/celles-là** |

**INTERROGATIVE PRONOUNS**

**LES PRONOMS INTERROGATIFS**

| | |
|---|---|
| which one | **lequel/laquelle** |
| which ones | **lesquels/lesquelles** |
| *Look at those pretty watches! Which ones do you prefer?* | *Regarde ces jolies montres! Lesquelles préfères-tu?* |

## Adjectives

## Les adjectifs

**DESCRIPTIVE ADJECTIVES**

**LES ADJECTIFS QUALIFICATIFS**

| | |
|---|---|
| *a new boss* | *un nouveau patron* |
| *a new student* | *un nouvel élève* |

 **Must-Know Tip**

Remember that the adjectives **beau, nouveau,** and **vieux,** which are to be placed before the noun, have two masculine singular forms. For instance, use **nouveau** before a consonant and **nouvel** before a vowel sound.

| | |
|---|---|
| *a brand new suit* | *un costume neuf* |
| *a brand new car* | *une voiture neuve* |

 **Must-Know Tip**

Remember that only a few adjectives (**beau, nouveau, vieux, jeune, joli, petit, grand, long, bon, mauvais, autre, même**) are placed before the noun. Most French adjectives are placed after the noun.

## INDEFINITE ADJECTIVES

each one

all

certain

*There is no correct answer.*

## INTERROGATIVE ADJECTIVES

which/what

*Which show are you watching?*

## LES ADJECTIFS INDÉFINIS

**chacun(e)**

**tout/toute/tous/toutes**

**certains/certaines**

**aucun(e)**

*Il n'y a aucune réponse correcte.*

## LES ADJECTIFS INTERROGATIFS

**quel/quels/quelle/quelles**

*Quelle émission regardes-tu?*

# Adverbs

currently

recently

rarely

regularly

sometimes

from time to time

always

never

already

finally

soon

later

today

yesterday

tomorrow

late

early

quickly

badly

well

*Today I do not feel well.*

better

# Les adverbes

**actuellement**

**récemment**

**rarement**

**régulièrement**

**quelquefois**

**de temps en temps**

**toujours**

**jamais**

**déjà**

**enfin**

**bientôt**

**plus tard**

**aujourd'hui**

**hier**

**demain**

**tard**

**tôt**

**vite**

**mal**

**bien**

*Aujourd'hui je me sens mal./*
*Aujourd'hui je ne me sens pas bien.*

**mieux**

| | |
|---|---|
| enough | **assez** |
| little | **peu** |
| a lot | **beaucoup** |
| too much | **trop** |
| very | **très** |
| here | **ici** |
| there | **là** |
| over there | **là-bas** |
| everywhere | **partout** |
| somewhere | **quelque part** |

## Interrogative Expressions

## Les locutions interrogatives

| | |
|---|---|
| how much/many | **combien (de)** |
| how | **comment** |
| what | **qu'est-ce que/que (qu')** |
| *What do you want?* | *Que veux-tu?/Qu'est-ce que tu veux?* |

 **Must-Know Tip**

Remember that you can ask a question either by using **est-ce que** before the subject and verb as in **"Est-ce que tu veux?"** ("*Do you want?*"), or by using an inversion as in **"Veux-tu?"**

| | |
|---|---|
| what | qu'est-ce qui |
| *What happened?* | *Qu'est-ce qui s'est passé?* |
| what | quoi |
| *with what* | *avec quoi* |
| when | quand |
| *since when* | *depuis quand* |
| *until when* | *jusqu'à quand* |
| where | où |
| *from where* | *d'où* |
| who | qui/qui est-ce qui |
| whom | qui est-ce que |

| | |
|---|---|
| *with whom* | *avec qui* |
| why | **pourquoi** |

# Letters, Invitations, and E-Mail

| **Letters** | **Les lettres** |
|---|---|
| address | l'adresse (f) |
| dear Jean-Claude/dear Marie | cher Jean-Claude/chère Marie |
| dear Sir/Madam | cher Monsieur/chère Madame |
| envelope | l'enveloppe (f) |
| express mail | service prioritaire d'envoi |
| letter | la lettre |
| mail | le courrier |
| package | le colis postal |
| postmark | le cachet de la poste |
| rate | le tarif |
| receive | recevoir |
| recipient | le destinataire |
| registered letter | la lettre recommandée |
| return receipt | l'avis de réception (m) |
| send/mail | envoyer/poster |
| sender | l'expéditeur (m) |
| *Sincerely* | *Veuillez agréer mes sentiments distingués* |
| stamp | le timbre |
| write | écrire |

 **Must-Know Tip**

Do not end a friendly letter with the literal translation of *Love* or *I love you*. Instead use one of the equivalents of *Your friend* or *Hugs and kisses*: **Amicalement, Bises, Bisous, Bons baisers, Je t'embrasse.**

| | |
|---|---|
| *Your friend* | *Amicalement* |
| zip code | **le code postal** |

## Invitations

## Invitations

| | |
|---|---|
| accept | **accepter** |
| announcement | **le faire-part** |
| bottle of wine | **une bouteille de vin** |
| celebration | **la fête** |
| ceremony/official function | **la cérémonie** |
| cocktail party | **le cocktail** |
| decline regretfully | **être au regret** |
| formal party | **la soirée** |
| gift | **le cadeau** |
| gladly | **volontiers** |
| *I gladly accept your invitation.* | *J'accepte volontiers votre invitation.* |
| *invite for a drink* | *inviter à prendre un pot* |
| please respond | **RSVP** |
| reception | **la réception** |
| sorry | **désolé(e)** |
| unfortunately | **malheureusement** |
| with pleasure | **avec plaisir** |

## E-Mail

## Le courrier électronique

| | |
|---|---|
| access | **l'accès (m)** |
| e-mail | **le courriel/mél/e-mail** |
| high-speed | **à haut débit** |
| *instant message* | *le message instantané* |
| Internet café | **le cybercafé** |
| Internet | **Internet, le Net** |
| log on | **se connecter** |
| password | **le mot de passe** |
| the Web | **le web** |
| *to send a message* | *envoyer un message* |

# 2

# *People and Relationships*

# Physical Description

## Face

face
*Her face is all red.*

## La figure

le visage/la figure
*Sa figure est toute rouge.*

 **Must-Know Tip**

Do not confuse **la figure** with the English word *figure*. **La figure** means *the face*. A person's figure is **la ligne**.

| | |
|---|---|
| complexion | **le teint** |
| pale | **pâle** |
| dark | **mat(e)** |
| tanned | **bronzé(e)** |
| freckles | **les points de rousseur** |
| mole | **le grain de beauté** |
| wrinkled | **ridé(e)** |

## Hair

| | |
|---|---|
| black | **noirs** |
| blond | **blonds** |
| brown | **châtains/bruns** |
| red | **roux/rousse** |

## Les cheveux

*My son has red hair.*
*Mon fils est roux.*

| | |
|---|---|
| curly | **bouclés** |
| long | **longs** |
| short | **courts** |
| straight | **raides** |

## Eyes

| | |
|---|---|
| almond-shaped | **en amande** |
| blue | **bleus** |

## Les yeux

| | |
|---|---|
| brown | **bruns** |
| green | **verts** |
| *He has brown hair and green eyes.* | *Il a les cheveux châtains et les yeux verts.* |
| hazel | **noisette** |
| round | **ronds** |
| shaped like slits/slanting | **bridés** |

## Nose

## Le nez

| | |
|---|---|
| aquiline | **aquilin** |
| flat/pug | **camus** |
| Roman | **romain** |
| turned up | **en trompette/retroussé** |
| wide | **large** |

## Lips

## Les lèvres

| | |
|---|---|
| fleshy | **charnues** |
| thick | **épaisses** |
| thin | **minces** |
| *He has a wide nose and very thin lips.* | *Il a le nez large et les lèvres très minces.* |

## Other Physical Traits

## Autres traits physiques

| | |
|---|---|
| muscular | **musclé(e)** |
| plump | **dodu(e)** |
| skinny | **maigrichon(ne)** |
| slender | **fluet(te)/élancé(e)** |
| small | **petit(e)** |
| stocky | **trapu(e)** |
| sturdy | **baraqué(e)** |
| tall | **grand(e)** |
| thin | **mince** |
| size | **la taille** |
| *His large size sets him apart.* | *Sa grande taille le distingue des autres.* |

| | |
|---|---|
| weigh | **peser** |
| weight | **le poids** |

# Character and Personality

| Descriptive Adjectives | Adjectifs qualificatifs |
|---|---|
| apathetic | **amorphe** |
| boring/annoying | **ennuyeux(-se)** |
| charismatic | **charismatique** |
| courageous | **courageux(-se)** |
| coward | **lâche** |
| creative | **créatif(-ve)** |
| cute | **mignon(ne)** |
| *This doll is cute.* | *Cette poupée est mignonne.* |
| discreet | **discret/discrète** |
| dishonest | **malhonnête** |
| energetic | **énergique** |
| extrovert | **extraverti(e)** |
| faithful | **fidèle** |
| hard-working | **travailleur(-se)** |
| honest | **honnête** |
| impatient | **impatient(e)** |
| indiscreet | **indiscret/indiscrète** |
| *Hush! Let's not be indiscreet!* | *Chut! Ne soyons pas indiscrets!* |
| ingenious | **ingénieux(-se)** |
| introvert | **introverti(e)** |
| lazy | **paresseux(-se)** |
| likeable | **sympathique** |
| loyal | **loyal(e)** |
| patient | **patient(e)** |
| persevering | **persévérant(e)** |
| playful | **enjoué(e)** |
| *This child is so playful!* | *Cet enfant est si enjoué!* |

| | |
|---|---|
| resourceful | **débrouillard(e)** |
| rough | **bourru(e)** |
| serious | **sérieux(-se)** |
| sociable | **sociable** |
| uncommunicative | **taciturne** |
| unfaithful | **infidèle** |
| unlikeable | **antipathique** |

## Descriptive Expressions / Locutions descriptives

| | |
|---|---|
| antisocial personality | **personnalité antisociale** |
| behavior | **le comportement** |
| character | **le caractère/la disposition/la personnalité** |
| *She has a strong personality.* | *Elle a du caractère.* |
| classy | **avoir de la classe** |
| daredevil | **le/la risque-tout/casse-cou** |
| generous | **avoir le cœur sur la main** |
| good/bad disposition | **bon/mauvais caractère** |
| happy-go-lucky | **bon vivant** |
| have a sense of humour | **avoir le sens de l'humour** |
| in a good/bad mood | **de bonne/mauvaise humeur** |
| mentality | **la mentalité** |
| paranoid | **paranoïaque** |
| *A paranoid person is afraid of everything.* | *Un paranoïaque a peur de tout.* |
| state of mind | **l'état d'esprit (m)** |
| temperament | **le tempérament** |
| trustworthy | **digne de foi** |

# Family Relationships and Family Activities

## Family Relationships / Relations familiales

| | |
|---|---|
| aunt | **la tante** |
| brother | **le frère** |

| | |
|---|---|
| daughter-in-law | **la brue** |
| father | **le père** |
| father-in-law/stepfather | **le beau-père** |
| female cousin | **la cousine** |
| fiancé/fiancée | **le/la fiancé(e)** |
| granddaughter | **la petite-fille** |
| grandson | **le petit-fils** |
| *My grandson's name is Alexander.* | ***Mon petit-fils s'appelle Alexandre.*** |
| half brother | **le demi-frère** |
| half sister | **la demi-sœur** |
| husband | **le mari** |
| male cousin | **le cousin** |
| mother | **la mère** |
| mother-in-law/stepmother | **la belle-mère** |
| *My stepmother is really beautiful.* | ***Ma belle-mère est vraiment belle.*** |
| nephew | **le neveu** |
| niece | **la nièce** |
| oldest child | **l'aîné(e)** |
| only child | **l'enfant unique (m/f)** |
| sister | **la sœur** |
| son-in-law | **le gendre** |
| stepdaughter | **la belle-fille** |
| stepson | **le beau-fils** |
| uncle | **l'oncle (m)** |
| wife | **la femme** |
| youngest child | **le/la cadet(te)** |
| *The oldest boy is fifteen; the youngest one is two.* | ***L'aîné a quinze ans; le cadet a deux ans.*** |

## Family Activities and Celebrations

## Activités et fêtes familiales

| | |
|---|---|
| eat a bite | **casser la croûte** |
| have a drink | **boire un pot** |

| | |
|---|---|
| *I am going to meet my cousins for a drink.* | *Je vais boire un pot avec mes cousins.* |
| marriage | **le mariage** |
| party/celebrate | **fêter/célébrer** |
| pay a visit | **rendre visite/faire une visite** |
| spend a vacation together | **passer des vacances ensemble** |
| watch children | **garder les enfants** |
| banquet/feast | **le festin** |
| baptism | **le baptême** |
| birth | **la naissance** |
| birthday | **l'anniversaire (m)** |
| cake | **le gâteau** |
| champagne | **le champagne** |
| congratulate | **féliciter** |
| drink to | **trinquer** |
| *Let's drink to her health!* | *Trinquons à sa santé!* |
| family celebration | **la fête de famille** |
| get together | **se réunir** |
| gift | **le cadeau/le présent** |
| Happy birthday! | **Bon anniversaire!** |
| Happy holidays! | **Joyeuses fêtes!** |
| Happy New Year! | **Bonne Année!** |
| honeymoon | **le voyage de noces/la lune de miel** |
| invite | **inviter** |
| offer one's wishes | **présenter ses vœux** |
| *Best wishes for a Happy New Year!* | *Mes meilleurs vœux pour une Bonne Année!* |
| propose a toast | **porter un toast** |
| wedding anniversary | **l'anniversaire de mariage (m)** |
| wedding | **le mariage/les noces (fpl)** |
| wine | **le vin** |
| wish | **souhaiter/faire des souhaits** |
| wish | **le souhait** |

# Nationalities, Ethnic Groups, and Religions

## Nationalities

### Nationalités

**NORTH AMERICAN**

**D'AMÉRIQUE DU NORD**

| American | américain(e) |
| Canadian | canadien(ne) |
| Cuban | cubain(e) |
| Dominican | dominicain(e) |
| Haitian | haïtien(ne) |

*I like primitive Haitian art very much.* — *L'art primitif haïtien me plaît beaucoup.*

| Mexican | mexicain(e) |
| Puerto Rican | portoricain(e) |

**CENTRAL AMERICAN**

**D'AMÉRIQUE CENTRALE**

| Costa Rican | costaricain(e) |
| Guatemalan | guatémalien(ne) |
| Honduran | hondurien(ne) |
| Nicaraguan | nicaraguen(ne) |
| Panamanian | panaménien(ne) |
| Salvadorian | salvadorien(ne) |

**SOUTH AMERICAN**

**D'AMÉRIQUE DU SUD**

| Argentinean | argentin(e) |

*Argentinean beef is among the best.* — *Le bœuf argentin est parmi les meilleurs.*

| Bolivian | bolivien(ne) |
| Brazilian | brésilien(ne) |
| Chilean | chiléen(ne) |
| Colombian | colombien(ne) |
| Ecuadoran | équatorien(ne)/équadorien(ne) |
| Paraguayan | paraguayen(ne) |
| Peruvian | péruvien(ne) |
| Uruguayan | uruguayen(ne) |
| Venezuelan | vénézuélien(ne) |

| **AFRICAN** | **AFRICAIN(E)** |
|---|---|
| Algerian | algérien(ne) |
| *I have an Algerian friend.* | *J'ai un ami algérien.* |
| Angolan | angolais(e) |
| Beninese | béninois(e) |
| Cameroonian | camerounais(e) |
| Congolese | congolais(e) |
| Egyptian | égyptien(ne) |
| Ethiopian | éthiopien(ne) |
| Gabonese | gabonais(e) |
| Ivorian | ivoirien(ne) |
| Jordanian | jordanien(ne) |
| Kenyan | kényan(e) |
| Lebanese | libanais(e) |
| Madagascan | malgache |
| *Do you know any Madagascan songs?* | *Connais-tu des chansons malgaches?* |
| Malian | malien(ne) |
| Mauritanian | mauritanien(ne) |
| Moroccan | marocain(e) |
| Senegalese | sénégalais(e) |
| Somalian | somalien(ne) |
| South African | sud-africain(e) |
| Sudanese | soudanais(e) |
| Togolese | togolais(e) |
| Tunisian | tunisien(ne) |

| **ASIAN** | **ASIATIQUE** |
|---|---|
| *I would like to visit some Asian countries this summer.* | *Je voudrais visiter des pays asiatiques cet été.* |
| Afghani | afgan(e) |
| Chinese | chinois(e) |
| Hindu | hindou(e) |
| Iranian | iranien(ne) |
| Iraqi | iraquien(ne) |
| Israeli | israélien(ne) |

| | |
|---|---|
| Japanese | **japonais(e)** |
| Korean | **coréen(ne)** |
| Palestinian | **palestinien(ne)** |
| Philippine | **philippin(e)** |
| Vietnamese | **vietnamien(ne)** |
| **EUROPEAN** | **EUROPÉEN(NE)** |
| Austrian | **autrichien(ne)** |
| Belgian | **belge** |
| *I love Belgian chocolate.* | ***J'adore le chocolat belge.*** |
| Bosnian | **bosniaque** |
| British | **britannique** |
| Croatian | **croate** |
| English | **anglais(e)** |
| Estonian | **estonien(ne)** |
| French | **français(e)** |
| *French cuisine is renowned.* | ***La cuisine française est renommée.*** |

 **Must-Know Tip**

Adjectives of nationality are not capitalized in French: **la cuisine française**. However, nouns describing people of a certain nationality are capitalized: **les Français**.

| | |
|---|---|
| Luxembourgian | **luxembourgeois(e)** |
| German | **allemand(e)** |
| Greek | **grec/greque** |
| Hungarian | **hongrois(e)** |
| Italian | **italien(ne)** |
| Polish | **polonais(e)** |
| Portuguese | **portugais(e)** |
| Romanian | **roumain(e)** |
| *The Romanian language is of Latin origin.* | ***La langue roumaine est d'origine latine.*** |

| | |
|---|---|
| Russian | **russe** |
| Slovakian | **slovaque** |
| Spanish | **espagnol(e)** |
| Swiss | **suisse** |
| Turkish | **turc/turque** |
| Ukrainian | **ukrainien(ne)** |

## Ethnic Groups / Les groupes éthniques

| | |
|---|---|
| African | **l'Africain(e)** |
| Asian | **l'Asiatique** |
| Jew/Israelite | **le juif/la juive, l'Israélite** |
| North African | **le/la Maghrébin(e)** |
| *There are lots of North Africans in France.* | *Il y a beaucoup de Maghrébins en France.* |

**Must-Know Tip**

Be aware that the term **Beur,** once a pejorative term, has become an acceptable and common description of young people of North African–Arab descent, born in France.

## Religions / Les religions

| | |
|---|---|
| Buddhism | **le bouddhisme** |
| Buddhist | **bouddhiste** |
| Catholicism | **le catholicisme** |
| Catholic | **catholique** |
| Christianity | **la christianité** |
| Christian | **chrétien(ne)** |
| Islam | **l'islam** |
| Muslim | **musulman(e)** |
| Judaism | **le judaïsme** |
| Jewish | **juif(-ve)** |

| Protestantism | le protestantisme |
| Protestant | protestant(e) |

# World Languages

## European Languages

## Les langues européennes

| Danish | le danois |
| Dutch | le hollandais |
| English | l'anglais |
| Finnish | le finois |
| French | le français |

*French is an official language at the United Nations.*

*Le français est une langue officielle aux Nations Unies.*

| German | l'allemand |
| Greek | le grec |
| Hungarian | le hongrois |
| Italian | l'italien |
| Norwegian | le norvégien |
| Polish | le polonais |
| Portuguese | le portugais |
| Russian | le russe |
| Spanish | l'espagnol |
| Swedish | le suédois |

## African Languages

## Les langues africaines

| Madagascan | le malgache |
| Swahili | le swahili |
| Arabic | l'arabe |

*Arabic and French are spoken in Tunisia, Morocco, and Algeria.*

*On parle arabe et français en Tunisie, au Maroc et en Algérie.*

## Asian Languages

## Les langues asiatiques

| Cantonese Chinese | le cantonais |
| Korean | le coréen |

| | |
|---|---|
| Japanese | **le japonais** |
| Laotian | **le laotien** |
| Mandarin Chinese | **le mandarin** |
| Vietnamese | **le vietnamien** |

# 3

# The Human Body, Health, and Medicine

# The Human Body

## General Terms

| | |
|---|---|
| artery | **l'artère (f)** |
| bile | **la bile** |
| blood | **le sang** |
| body | **le corps** |
| bone | **l'os (m)** |
| collar bone | **la clavicule** |
| cranium | **le crâne** |
| muscle | **le muscle** |
| nerve | **le nerf** |
| rib | **la côte** |
| *I broke a rib while skiing.* | ***Je me suis cassé une côte en skiant.*** |
| rib cage | **la cage thoracique** |
| skeleton | **le squelette** |
| spinal column | **la colonne vertébrale** |
| tendon | **le tendon** |
| vein | **la veine** |
| vertebra | **la vertèbre** |

## Généralités

## Senses

| | |
|---|---|
| achy | **avoir mal** |
| cold | **avoir froid** |
| hot | **avoir chaud** |
| hungry | **avoir faim** |
| thirsty | **avoir soif** |
| sleepy | **avoir sommeil** |

## Les sens

 **Must-Know Tip**

Remember to use the verb **avoir** with sensations such as *being cold, hot, hungry, thirsty, sleepy, achy*. "*I am cold*" is translated as "**J'ai froid.**"

| | |
|---|---|
| bitter | **amer/amère** |
| feel | **se sentir** |
| *Do you feel well?* | ***Tu te sens bien?*** |
| hear | **entendre** |
| hearing | **l'ouïe (f)** |
| listen | **écouter** |
| salty | **salé(e)** |
| see | **voir** |
| sense of smell | **l'odorat (m)** |
| sight | **la vue** |
| smell | **sentir** |
| *Roses smell good!* | ***Les roses sentent bon!*** |

 **Must-Know Tip**

Remember that many verbs like **sentir** can be used reflexively or nonreflexively. **Sentir** means *to smell*, whereas **se sentir** means *to feel*. Another example is **coucher le bébé**, which means *to put the baby to sleep*, whereas **se coucher** means *to go to sleep*.

| | |
|---|---|
| smell | **l'odeur (f)** |
| sweet | **sucré(e)** |
| tactile | **tactile** |
| taste | **goûter** |
| taste | **le goût** |
| touch | **toucher** |
| touch | **le toucher** |

## Head and Face  ## La tête et le visage

| | |
|---|---|
| brain | **le cerveau** |
| cheek | **la joue** |
| chin | **le menton** |
| ear | **l'oreille (f)** |

| | |
|---|---|
| eye (eyes) | l'œil (m) (les yeux) |
| *It costs an arm and a leg.* | *Ça coûte les yeux de la tête.* |

 **Must-Know Tip**

Remember that many familiar everyday life expressions in French refer to parts of the body; these cannot be translated literally. *"J'ai une dent contre lui"* means *"I hold a grudge against him."*

| | |
|---|---|
| eyebrow | **le sourcil** |
| eyelash | **le cil** |
| eyelid | **la paupière** |
| forehead | **le front** |
| neck (nape) | **la nuque** |
| neck | **le cou** |
| nose | **le nez** |
| pimple | **le bouton** |
| pupil (eye) | **la pupille (de l'œil)** |
| skull | **le crâne** |
| throat | **la gorge** |
| *I have a sore throat.* | *J'ai mal à la gorge.* |
| tongue | **la langue** |
| wrinkle | **la ride** |

## Mouth

## La bouche

| | |
|---|---|
| baby tooth | **la dent de lait** |
| canine tooth | **la canine** |
| incisor | **l'incisive (f)** |
| jaw | **la mâchoire** |
| lip | **la lèvre** |
| molar | **la molaire** |
| palate | **le palais** |
| tongue | **la langue** |
| tonsils | **les amygdales** |

| | |
|---|---|
| *He has inflamed tonsils.* | *Il a les amygdales enflammées.* |
| tooth | **la dent** |
| wisdom tooth | **la dent de sagesse** |

## Torso

## Le torse

| | |
|---|---|
| back | **le dos** |
| belly | **le ventre** |
| belly button | **le nombril** |
| bladder | **la vessie** |
| bottom/buttocks | **le derrière/les fesses (fpl)** |
| breast | **le sein** |
| chest | **la poitrine** |
| heart | **le cœur** |
| intestine | **l'intestin (m)** |
| kidney | **le rein** |
| *He needs a kidney transplant.* | *Il lui faut une greffe de rein.* |
| liver | **le foie** |
| lung | **le poumon** |
| organ | **l'organe (m)** |
| pancreas | **le pancréas** |
| penis | **le pénis** |
| stomach | **l'estomac (m)** |
| vagina | **le vagin** |
| waist | **la taille** |

## Limbs

## Les membres

### ARM AND HAND

### LE BRAS ET LA MAIN

| | |
|---|---|
| armpit | **l'aisselle (f)** |
| elbow | **le coude** |
| *She hurt her elbow while playing tennis.* | *Elle s'est fait mal au coude en jouant au tennis.* |
| finger | **le doigt** |
| fingernail | **l'ongle (m)** |
| fist | **le poing** |

| | |
|---|---|
| forearm | l'avant-bras (m) |
| index finger | l'index (m) |
| knuckle | l'articulation du doigt (f) |
| knucklebone | l'osselet (m) |
| shoulder | l'épaule (f) |
| thumb | le pouce |
| wrist | le poignet |
| *She wears three bracelets on her left wrist.* | *Elle porte trois bracelets au poignet gauche.* |

| **LEG AND FOOT** | **LA JAMBE ET LE PIED** |
|---|---|
| Achilles' heel | le talon d'Achille |
| ankle | la cheville |
| blister | l'ampoule (f) |
| boil | le furoncle |
| bunion | l'oignon (m) |
| corn | le cor |
| hip | la hanche |
| knee | le genou |
| thigh | la cuisse |
| toe | l'orteil (m)/le doigt de pied |

# Health and Hygiene

## Health

## La santé

| | |
|---|---|
| fit | en forme |
| *She is in top shape.* | *Elle est en pleine forme.* |
| fitness | la forme |
| healthy | en bonne santé |
| look good | avoir bonne mine |
| mental health | la santé mentale |
| prevent | prévenir/éviter |
| preventive medicine | la médecine préventive |
| robust | robuste |

| strength | la force |
| vigor | la vigueur |
| *He preserved his vigor through the years.* | *Il a conservé sa vigueur au cours des années.* |
| well-being | le bien-être |

## Personal Hygiene / L'hygiène personnelle

| bath | le bain |
| bath salts | les sels de bain |
| bathe | se baigner |
| bathtub | la baignoire |
| body odor | l'odeur corporelle (f) |
| clean | propre |
| *This is a clean room.* | *C'est une chambre propre.* |

 **Must-Know Tip**

Remember to use the adjective **propre** after the noun if you want it to mean *clean*. Used before the noun as in "**ma propre chambre**," it will mean "*my own room.*"

| cleanliness | la propreté |
| cleansing cream | la crème lavante |
| cologne | l'eau de Cologne (f) |
| deodorant | le déodorant |
| fleas | les puces (fpl) |
| groom | faire sa toilette |
| hand lotion | la crème pour les mains |
| perfume | l'eau de toilette (f)/le parfum |
| lipstick | le rouge à lèvres |
| lotion | la lotion |
| menstruation | les règles (fpl)/la menstruation |
| moisturizer | la crème hydratante |

| | |
|---|---|
| *In this dry climate, you must use moisturizers.* | *Dans ce climat sec, il faut se servir de crème hydratante.* |
| put on makeup | **se maquiller** |
| sanitary pad | **la serviette hygiénique** |
| shower | **la douche** |
| shower | **prendre une douche** |
| skin foundation | **le fond de teint** |
| soap | **le savon** |
| sponge | **l'éponge (f)** |
| sweat | **la sueur** |
| tampon | **le tampon hygiénique** |
| toilet paper | **le papier hygiénique** |
| towel | **la serviette** |
| wash | **(se) laver** |
| *Wash your hands!* | *Lave-toi les mains!* |
| washcloth | **le gant de toilette** |

 **Must-Know Tip**

Remember to use the definite articles **le, la, l', les** before a part of the body, especially with reflexive verbs, as in "*Je me brosse les cheveux.*"

## Hair, Nails, and Teeth

## Cheveux, poils, ongles et dents

**HAIR CARE**

**SOINS DES CHEVEUX ET DES POILS**

| | |
|---|---|
| bald | **chauve** |
| baldness | **la calvitie** |
| beard | **la barbe** |
| beauty salon | **le salon de coiffure** |
| dandruff | **les pellicules (fpl)** |
| hair (body) | **le poil** |

| hair (head) | **les cheveux (mpl)** |
| *brush one's hair* | *se brosser les cheveux* |
| *comb one's hair* | *se peigner les cheveux* |
| *get a haircut* | *se faire couper les cheveux* |
| *dry one's hair* | *se sécher les cheveux* |
| *style one's hair* | *se coiffer* |
| hair stylist | **le coiffeur/la coiffeuse** |
| hairbrush | **la brosse** |
| haircut | **la coupe de cheveux** |
| lather | **la mousse** |
| lice | **les poux (mpl)** |
| mustache | **la moustache** |
| pluck eyebrows | **s'épiler les sourcils** |
| shampoo | **le shampooing** |
| shave | **(se) raser** |
| wax | **la cire (épilatoire)** |

**NAIL CARE**          **SOINS DES ONGLES**

| file one's nails | **se limer les ongles** |
| nail clippers | **les ciseaux à ongles (mpl)** |
| nail file | **la lime à ongles** |
| nail polish | **le vernis à ongles** |
| nail polish remover | **le dissolvant** |
| manicure | **la manucure** |
| pedicure | **le soin des pieds** |
| pedicure professional | **le/la pédicure** |

 **Must-Know Tip**

Be aware that although **la manucure** can describe hand and nail care, the same word (**le/la manucure**) is also used for the professional who administers the care. The term **le/la pédicure** refers to the person who administers foot care.

| ORAL HYGIENE | L'HYGIÈNE DENTAIRE |
|---|---|
| brush one's teeth | **se brosser les dents** |
| floss | **le fil dentaire** |
| gargle | **se rincer la gorge** |
| tooth decay | **la carie** |
| tooth plaque | **le tartre** |
| toothbrush | **la brosse à dents** |
| toothpaste | **la pâte dentifrice** |
| toothpick | **le cure-dents** |

# Illnesses, Disabilities, and Medical Care

## Illnesses and Medical Conditions

## Les maladies et les conditions médicales

| GENERAL TERMS | GÉNÉRALITÉS |
|---|---|
| accident | **l'accident (m)** |
| become ill | **tomber malade** |
| bleed | **saigner** |
| blood | **le sang** |
| breathless | **à bout d'haleine** |
| broken | **cassé(e)** |
| bruise | **le bleu** |
| burn | **la brûlure** |
| choke | **s'étrangler** |
| convalescent | **convalescent(e)** |
| discomfort | **le malaise** |
| dizzy | **pris(e) d'étourdissement** |
| drowsiness | **la somnolence** |
| drowsy | **somnolent(e)** |
| faint | **s'évanouir/défaillir** |
| *A big scare makes her faint.* | *Une grande peur la fait défaillir.* |
| fall | **la chute** |

| feel faint | se sentir défaillant(e) |
| fracture | la fracture |
| get better/recover | se remettre |
| hurt (oneself) | (se) faire mal |
| *Where does it hurt?* | *Où est-ce que ça fait mal?* |
| ill/sick | malade |
| looking sick | avoir mauvaise mine |
| injured person | le/la blessé(e) |
| injury | la blessure |
| nauseated | avoir la nausée |
| pain | la douleur |
| patient | le/la patient(e) |
| queasiness | le mal de cœur |

 **Must-Know Tip**

Remember not to use the expression **le mal de cœur** to refer to the heart.
It means nothing more than queasiness.

| recuperate | récupérer |
| relapse | la rechute |
| relapse | faire une rechute |
| sprain | la foulure/l'entorse |
| *This horse will not compete in the race. He has a sprain.* | *Ce cheval ne participera pas à la course. Il a une entorse.* |
| suffer | souffrir |
| suffering | la souffrance |
| suffocate | s'asphyxier |
| swelling | l'enflure (f) |
| swollen | enflé(e) |
| unconscious | inconscient(e) |
| *under the weather* | *malade/indisposé(e)* |
| weak | faible |

| weaken | s'affaiblir |
| worsen | empirer/s'aggraver |
| *Her condition is worsening.* | *Son état s'aggrave.* |
| wound | la blessure/la plaie |

### COLDS AND GASTROINTESTINAL AILMENTS

### RHUMES ET SOUFFRANCES GASTRO-INTESTINALES

| chill/cold | le refroidissement/le rhume |
| colic | la colique |
| constipated | constipé(e) |
| constipation | la constipation |
| cough | la toux |
| cough | tousser |
| diarrhea | la diarrhée |
| earache | le mal d'oreille |
| fever | la fièvre |
| flu | la grippe |
| *Take the flu shot!* | *Fais-toi vacciner contre la grippe!* |
| food poisoning | l'intoxication alimentaire (f) |
| indigestion | l'indigestion (f)/la crise de foie |
| infection | l'infection (f) |
| middle ear infection | l'otite (f) |
| migraine | la migraine |
| sneeze | éternuer |
| sweat/perspire | transpirer |
| upset stomach | le mal de ventre |
| vomit | vomir |

## Chronic or Life-Threatening Disorders

## Les afflictions chroniques ou sérieuses

### CHRONIC DISORDERS

### LES AFFLICTIONS CHRONIQUES

| acne | l'acné (f) |
| *The dermatologist gave him a cream for acne.* | *Le dermatologue lui a donné une crème contre l'acné.* |
| AIDS | le sida |

| | |
|---|---|
| allergy | l'allergie (f) |
| arthritis | l'arthrite (f) |
| asthma | l'asthme (m) |
| attention deficit | le déficit d'attention |
| blood pressure | la pression artérielle |
| bronchitis | la bronchite |
| diabetes | le diabète |
| herpes | l'herpès (m) |
| high blood pressure | l'hypertension (f) |
| jaundice | la jaunisse |
| joint ache/stiffness | la courbature |
| *I have a stiff back.* | *J'ai une courbature dans le dos.* |
| rheumatism | le rhumatisme |
| scoliosis | la scoliose |

| **LIFE-THREATENING DISORDERS** | **LES AFFLICTIONS SÉRIEUSES** |
|---|---|
| appendicitis | l'appendicite (f) |
| cancer | le cancer |
| chicken pox | la varicelle |
| German measles | la rubéole |
| heart attack | l'infarctus (m)/la crise cardiaque |
| hemophilia | l'hémophilie (f) |
| HIV positive | séropositif(-ve) |
| leukemia | la leucémie |
| *One day leukemia will be eradicated.* | *Un jour la leucémie sera éradiquée.* |
| measles | la rougeole |
| meningitis | la méningite |
| mumps | les oreillons (mpl) |
| pneumonia | la pneumonie |
| tuberculosis | la tuberculose |

# Psychological Conditions and Addictions

# Les problèmes psychologiques et la dépendance

| | |
|---|---|
| alcohol | l'alcool (m) |
| alcoholic | l'alcoolique (m/f) |

| | |
|---|---|
| alcoholism | l'alcoolisme (m) |
| anorexia | l'anorexie (f) |
| bulimia | la boulimie |
| depressed | déprimé(e) |
| depression | la dépression |
| drug addict | le/la drogué(e) |
| *The drug addict is in a rehabilitation center.* | *Le drogué est dans un centre de réhabilitation.* |
| drug addiction | la dépendance/la toxicomanie |
| drug | la drogue/le stupéfiant |
| hooked | accro |
| insane | aliéné(e)/dérangé(e) |
| insane | fou/folle |
| mental illness | la maladie mentale |
| neurosis | la neurose |
| nicotine | la nicotine |
| paranoia | la paranoïa |
| stress | le stress |
| *Stress contributes to many illnesses.* | *Le stress contribue à beaucoup de maladies.* |
| tobacco addiction | le tabagisme |
| withdrawal symptom | le symptôme de retrait |

## Disabilities / Les infirmités

| | |
|---|---|
| amputee | l'amputé(e) |
| blind | aveugle |
| deaf | sourd(e) |
| deaf-mute | sourd(e)-muet(te) |
| deafness | la surdité |
| deficiency | la déficience |
| *A pilot cannot have a visual deficiency.* | *Un pilote ne peut pas souffrir d'une déficience visuelle.* |
| disability | l'incapacité (f)/l'infirmité (f) |
| handicapped | handicapé(e) |

| | |
|---|---|
| invalid | **infirme/invalide** |
| lame | **boiteux(-se)** |
| limp | **boiter** |
| mute | **muet(te)** |
| paralysis | **la paralysie** |
| paralyzed | **paralysé(e)** |
| *He is paralyzed because of a road* *accident.* | *Il est paralysé à la suite d'un accident* *de la route.* |
| paraplegic | **paraplégique** |

## Medical Care

## Les soins médicaux

| GENERAL TERMS | GÉNÉRALITÉS |
|---|---|
| anesthetic | **l'anesthésie (f)** |
| antibiotic | **l'antibiotique (m)** |
| aspirin | **l'aspirine (f)** |
| bandage | **le bandage** |
| small bandage | **le pansement** |
| birth control pill | **la pillule contraceptive** |
| blood test | **l'analyse de sang (f)** |
| blood transfusion | **la transfusion (sanguine)** |
| check | **ausculter** |
| checkup | **l'auscultation (f)** |
| *They have free checkups at the clinic.* | *On donne des auscultations gratuites* *à la clinique.* |
| clinic | **la clinique** |
| consultation | **la consultation** |
| cough medicine | **le sirop pour la toux** |
| critical | **grave** |
| diagnosis | **le diagnostic** |
| drops | **les gouttes (fpl)** |
| drug/medication | **le médicament** |
| electrocardiogram (EKG) | **l'électrocardiogramme (m)** |
| emergency | **l'urgence (f)** |

| | |
|---|---|
| *In case of emergency, call the Medical Health Emergency Service* | *En cas d'urgence, appelez le Service d'Aide Médicale d'Urgence.* |
| examination | **l'examen médical (m)** |
| first aid | **les premiers soins** |
| first-aid kit | **le kit de secours** |
| hospital | **l'hôpital (m)** |
| injection | **la piqûre** |
| laxative | **le laxatif** |
| medical insurance | **l'assurance médicale (f)** |
| *Do you have medical insurance?* | *Avez-vous une assurance médicale?* |
| medication | **le médicament** |
| ointment | **la pommade** |
| operation | **l'opération (f)** |
| pill | **la pillule/le cachet** |
| prescription | **l'ordonnance (f)** |
| rest | **le repos** |
| rest | **se reposer** |
| resuscitation | **la ressuscitation/réanimation** |
| sonogram | **l'échographie (f)** |
| tablet | **le comprimé** |
| *The nurse gave me a tablet.* | *L'infirmière m'a donné un comprimé.* |
| therapy | **la thérapie** |
| transplant | **la greffe** |
| treatment | **le traitement** |
| urine test | **l'examen d'urine (m)** |
| vaccinate | **vacciner** |
| *The baby has been vaccinated.* | *Le bébé a été vacciné.* |
| vaccine | **le vaccin** |
| wheelchair | **le fauteuil roulant/la chaise roulante** |
| x-ray | **la radiographie** |
| **DENTAL CARE** | **LES SOINS DENTAIRES** |
| abscess | **l'abcès (m)** |
| braces | **l'appareil dentaire (m)** |

| cavity | la dent cariée |
| *I have one cavity.* | *J'ai une dent cariée.* |
| dental crown | la couronne |
| denture | le dentier |
| filling | le plombage |
| pull | arracher |
| toothache | le mal de dent |

### EYE CARE
### LES SOINS OCULAIRES

| contact lens | la lentille de contact |
| *disposable contact lenses* | *des lentilles de contact jetables* |
| *permanent contact lenses* | *des lentilles de contact de port permanent* |
| cross-eyed | affecté(e) de strabisme |
| (be) cross-eyed | loucher |
| *Poor little one; she is cross-eyed.* | *La pauvre petite; elle louche.* |
| eyeglasses | les lunettes |
| nearsightedness | la myopie |
| nearsighted | myope |

## Health Specialists and Facilities
## Les spécialistes et les services de la santé

### SPECIALISTS
### LES SPÉCIALISTES

| anesthesiologist | l'anesthésiste (m/f) |
| cardiologist | le/la cardiologue |
| chiropractor | le/la chiropracticien(ne) |
| dental hygienist | l'hygiéniste dentaire (m/f) |
| dental surgeon | le/la chirurgien(ne) dentaire |
| dentist | le/la dentiste |
| dermatologist | le/la dermatologue |
| doctor/physician | le médecin/le docteur |
| *The doctor has many patients.* | *Le médecin a beaucoup de patients.* |
| emergency room doctor | le médecin urgentiste |

| | |
|---|---|
| endocrinologist | l'endocrinologiste/ l'endocrinologue (m/f) |
| first-aid worker | le/la secouriste |
| gastroenterology specialist | le/la spécialiste en gastro-entérologie |
| general practitioner | le/la généraliste |
| geriatrics specialist | le/la spécialiste en gériatrie |
| gynecologist | le/la gynécologue |
| heart specialist | le/la cardiologue |
| homeopath | l'homéopathe (m/f) |
| intern | l'interne (m/f) |
| *Interns work long hours.* | *Les internes travaillent de longues heures.* |
| midwife | la sage-femme |
| neurologist | le/la neurologue |
| nurse | l'infirmier/l'infirmière |
| nurse's aide | l'aide-soignant(e) |
| nutritionist | le/la diététicien(ne) |
| oncologist | l'oncologue (m/f) |
| ophthalmologist | l'ophtalmologiste (m/f) |
| optician | l'opticien(ne) |
| optometrist | l'oculiste (m/f) |
| *My optometrist recommends glasses.* | *Mon oculiste me recommande des lunettes.* |
| orthopedic surgeon | le/la chirurgien(ne) orthopédiste |
| paramedic | l'ambulancier (m) |
| pediatrician | le/la pédiatre |
| pharmacist | le/la pharmacien(ne) |
| physical therapist | le/la kinésithérapeute |
| physician | le médecin |
| physician's assistant | le médecin assistant |
| plastic surgeon | le/la chirurgien(ne) esthétique |
| *This plastic surgeon is reputed.* | *Ce chirurgien plastique est réputé.* |

| | |
|---|---|
| podiatrist | **le/la podologiste** |
| practical nurse | **l'aide-soignant(e)** |
| psychiatrist | **le/la psychiatre** |
| psychologist | **le/la psychologue** |
| radiologist | **le/la radiologue** |
| researcher | **le chercheur/la chercheuse** |
| resident | **le médecin-assistant** |
| specialist | **le/la spécialiste** |
| surgeon | **le/la chirurgien(ne)** |
| therapist | **le/la thérapiste** |
| urologist | **l'urologiste/l'urologue (m/f)** |
| veterinarian | **le/la vétérinaire** |
| *It is time to take Fido to the vet.* | ***Il est temps qu'on amène Fido chez le vétérinaire.*** |
| x-ray technician | **le/la technicien(ne) radiologique** |

| **FACILITIES** | **LES SERVICES** |
|---|---|
| ambulance | **l'ambulance (f)** |
| clinic | **la clinique** |
| doctor's office | **le cabinet** |
| emergency room | **la salle des urgences** |
| hospital | **l'hôpital (m)** |
| infirmary | **l'infirmerie (f)** |
| intensive care unit (ICU) | **les services de soins intensifs (mpl)** |
| office hours | **les heures d'ouverture (fpl)** |
| on call | **de garde** |
| *My doctor is on call this weekend.* | ***Mon médecin est de garde ce week-end.*** |
| operating room | **la salle d'opération** |
| outpatient clinic | **la clinique ambulatoire** |
| pharmacy | **la pharmacie** |
| private room | **la chambre particulière** |
| waiting room | **la salle d'attente** |

# Life and Death

## Stages of Life

adolescence

adulthood

age

*He is at an age to know right from wrong.*

artificial insemination

baby

be born

birth certificate

birth

birthday

born

childhood

creation

give birth

infancy

legally responsible

*At eighteen years of age, you are legally responsible.*

life

live

maternity

middle age

minor

newborn

old

old age

paternity

people

pregnancy

## Les diverses étapes de la vie

l'adolescence (f)

l'âge adulte (m)

l'âge (m)

*Il a l'âge de raison.*

l'insémination artificielle (f)

le bébé

naître

le certificat de naissance

la naissance

l'anniversaire (m)

né(e)

l'enfance (f)

la création

accoucher

le bas âge

majeur(e)

*À l'âge de dix-huit ans, on est majeur.*

la vie

vivre

la maternité

l'âge mûr (m)

le/la mineur(e)

le/la nouveau-né(e)

vieux/vieille

la vieillesse/le troisième âge

la paternité

les gens/les personnes

la grossesse

| | |
|---|---|
| pregnant | **enceinte** |
| premature | **prématuré(e)** |
| prime of life | **la fleur de l'âge** |
| *He is in the prime of life.* | *Il est à la fleur de l'âge.* |
| puberty | **la puberté** |
| young | **jeune** |
| youth | **la jeunesse** |

## Death      La mort

| | |
|---|---|
| afterlife | **l'au-delà** |
| body | **le corps** |
| burial | **l'enterrement (m)** |
| bury | **enterrer** |
| cadaver | **le cadavre** |
| cemetery | **le cimetière** |
| condolences | **les condoléances (fpl)** |
| *I want to express my condolences.* | *Je tiens à exprimer mes condoléances.* |
| cremated | **incinéré(e)** |
| cremation | **l'incinération (f)** |
| death certificate | **le certificat de décès** |
| deceased | **décédé(e)** |
| die | **mourir** |
| epitaph | **l'épitaphe (f)** |
| funeral home | **le service des pompes funèbres** |
| funerals | **les funérailles (fpl)** |
| grave | **la sépulture** |
| *I visited Chopin's grave in Paris.* | *J'ai visité la sépulture de Chopin à Paris.* |
| hearse | **le corbillard** |
| heir | **l'héritier/l'héritière** |
| inheritance | **l'héritage (m)** |
| inherit | **hériter** |
| interment | **l'inhumation (f)** |
| last rites | **les rites funéraires (mpl)** |

| | |
|---|---|
| life insurance policy | **la police d'assurance vie** |
| mourn | **être en deuil** |
| mourning | **le deuil** |
| obituary | **l'obituaire (m)** |
| pass away | **trépasser** |
| reincarnation | **la réincarnation (f)** |
| tomb | **la tombe** |
| tombstone | **la pierre tombale** |
| wake | **la veille** |
| will | **le testament** |

**4**

# *Education*

# School Subjects

## Elementary School

arts and crafts
counting
dancing
drawing
first grade
second and third grades
fourth and fifth grades
kindergarten


learn
mental calculation
pasting
*Little children love pasting.*
reading
singing
spelling
vocabulary
writing

## Middle School and High School

algebra
anatomy
art
*I am taking an Introduction to Art class.*

biology
calculus
chemistry
civics
classical languages

## Le cycle élémentaire

le travail manuel
compter
la danse
le dessin
le cours préparatoire
le cours élémentaire
le cours moyen
l'école maternelle/le jardin d'enfants

apprendre
le calcul mental
le collage
*Les petits adorent le collage.*
la lecture
le chant
l'orthographe (f)
le vocabulaire
l'écriture (f)

## Le cycle secondaire

l'algèbre (f)
l'anatomie (f)
l'art (m)
*Je suis un cours d'Introduction à l'Art.*

la biologie
le calcul infinitésimal
la chimie
l'instruction civique (f)
les langues classiques (fpl)

| composition | **la composition/rédaction** |
| computer science | **l'informatique (f)** |
| course | **le cours** |
| debate | **le débat** |
| discussion | **la discussion** |
| *Discussion is important in class.* | *La discussion est importante en cours.* |
| earth science | **les sciences naturelles** |
| essay | **la dissertation** |
| geography | **la géographie** |
| geometry | **la géométrie** |
| grammar | **la grammaire** |
| gymnastics | **la gymnastique** |
| high school | **le lycée** |
| history | **l'histoire (f)** |
| literature | **la littérature** |
| mathematics | **les mathématiques (fpl)** |
| middle school | **le collège** |

 **Must-Know Tip**

Be aware that **collège** is a false cognate as it means *middle school*. To say *college*, use the word **université**.

| modern language | **la langue moderne** |
| *I study two modern languages.* | *J'étudie deux langues modernes.* |
| music | **la musique** |
| outdoor sports | **les sports en plein air (mpl)** |
| philosophy | **la philosophie** |
| physical education | **l'éducation physique (f)** |
| physics | **la physique** |
| psychology | **la psychologie** |
| science | **la science** |
| *Earth science is required.* | *Les sciences naturelles sont obligatoires.* |

| | |
|---|---|
| social science | **les sciences sociales** |
| space science | **les sciences de l'espace** |
| summary | **le résumé** |
| team sports | **les sports d'équipe (mpl)** |
| text analysis | **l'explication de texte (f)** |
| trigonometry | **la trigonométrie** |

## Vocational School / Le lycée professionnel

| | |
|---|---|
| accounting | **la comptabilité** |
| agriculture school | **l'école agricole (f)** |
| construction trade school | **la formation professionnelle des métiers du bâtiment** |
| culinary services | **l'alimentation (f)** |
| fashion | **la mode** |
| forestry and landscaping school | **l'école des métiers de la terre et de la nature** |
| hospitality school | **l'école hôtelière (f)** |
| pharmaceutical school | **l'école de laborantins médicaux (f)** |
| sales and management | **la vente et la gestion** |
| secretarial occupations | **le secrétariat** |
| *She plans to be a secretary.* | *Elle se destine au secrétariat.* |
| service industry | **services et conseils (mpl)** |
| technical school | **l'école technique (f)** |
| trade school | **l'école de commerce/l'école commerciale (f)** |
| training | **la formation** |
| vocational training center | **le centre de formation professionnelle** |

# In the Classroom

## Materials and Supplies / Matériel et fournitures scolaires

| | |
|---|---|
| binder | **le classeur** |
| board | **le tableau** |

| | |
|---|---|
| book | **le livre/le bouquin** |
| calculator | **la calculatrice** |
| CD player | **le lecteur de CD** |
| computer | **l'ordinateur** |
| dictionary | **le dictionnaire** |
| DVD player | **le lecteur de DVD** |
| eraser (for the board) | **l'éponge (f)** |
| *Take the eraser and clean the board!* | ***Prends l'éponge et efface le tableau!*** |
| eraser (pencil) | **la gomme** |
| folder | **le classeur** |
| handout | **la copie** |
| map | **la carte** |
| marker | **le feutre** |
| notebook | **le cahier** |
| paper | **le papier** |
| pen | **le stylo** |
| pencil sharpener | **le taille-crayon** |
| pencil | **le crayon** |
| projector | **le projecteur** |
| *Here are the transparencies. Where is the projector?* | ***Voici les transparents. Où est le projecteur?*** |
| protractor | **le rapporteur** |
| ruler | **la règle** |
| sheet | **la feuille** |
| student desk | **le pupitre** |
| teacher's desk | **le bureau** |
| television | **la télévision** |
| VCR | **le magnétoscope** |
| workbook | **le manuel** |

## Class Structures and Activities / Structures et activités scolaires

| | |
|---|---|
| answer | **répondre** |
| apply oneself | **faire des efforts/s'appliquer** |
| ask | **demander/interroger** |

| | |
|---|---|
| average | **la moyenne** |
| cheat | **tricher** |
| *Cheating is forbidden.* | ***Il est défendu de tricher.*** |
| copy | **copier** |
| correct | **corriger** |
| cut class | **sécher le cours** |
| disobey | **désobéir** |
| elective subject | **la matière facultative** |
| exam | **l'examen (m)** |
| exercise | **l'exercice (m)** |
| explain | **expliquer** |
| fail | **rater/échouer** |
| grade | **la note** |
| grade | **noter** |
| *All my essays are graded.* | ***Toutes mes dissertations sont notées.*** |
| group work | **le travail de groupe** |
| homework | **les devoirs (mpl)** |
| lesson | **la leçon** |
| listen | **écouter** |
| major subject | **la matière principale** |
| make progress | **faire des progrès** |
| participate | **participer** |
| principal | **le principal/directeur; la principale/directrice** |
| quiz | **l'interro (f)/l'interrogation (f)/la colle/le contrôle** |
| *Every Friday we have a quiz.* | ***Tous les vendredis, nous avons une interro.*** |
| read | **lire** |
| repeat a grade level | **redoubler** |
| report card | **le bulletin scolaire** |
| required subject | **la matière obligatoire** |
| skip school | **faire l'école buissonnière** |
| skip a class | **sécher un cours** |

| student | l'élève (m/f)/l'étudiant(e) |
| substitute | le/la remplaçant(e); le/la surveillant(e) |
| succeed/pass a course | réussir un cours |
| take an exam | passer un examen |

 **Must-Know Tip**

Be aware that **passer un examen** does not mean *to pass an exam*. It simply means *to take an exam*.

| take notes | prendre des notes |
| *Taking notes helps you remember.* | *Prendre des notes vous aide à vous rappeler.* |
| teacher (pre-K and elementary) | le maître/la maîtresse, l'instituteur (m)/l'institutrice (f) |
| teacher (other than pre-K and elementary) | le professeur |

 **Must-Know Tip**

Be aware that **l'instituteur** is used for an elementary school teacher, whereas **le professeur** is used for middle school, high school, and college teachers.

| understand | comprendre |
| write | écrire |

## Technology

## La technologie

| audiocassette | la cassette audio |
| calculator | la calculatrice |
| CD-ROM | le CD-ROM |

| computer | l'ordinateur (m) |
|---|---|
| DVD player | le lecteur de DVD |
| DVD | le DVD |
| headphones | le casque |
| *In the language lab, we wear headphones.* | *Dans le labo de langue, on porte des casques.* |
| information highway | l'autoroute informatique (f) |
| interactive presentation | la présentation interactive |
| laptop | l'ordinateur portatif (m) |
| microphone | le microphone |
| printer | l'imprimante (f) |
| scanner | le scanneur/le scanner |
| smart board | le tableau blanc interactif |
| tape player | le magnétophone |
| television set | le téléviseur/la télévision |
| VCR | le magnétoscope |
| *The VCR is in the TV set.* | *Le magnétoscope est intégré à la télé.* |
| videocassette | la cassette vidéo |
| videoconference | la vidéoconférence |
| wireless technology | la technologie réseau sans fil |

# University Studies and Long-Distance Learning

## Higher Education / Le cycle universitaire

| admitted | reçu(e) |
|---|---|
| bachelor's degree | la licence |
| course credit | l'unité de valeur (f) |
| directed studies | les cours dirigés (mpl) |
| discipline/field | la discipline |
| enrolled | inscrit(e) |
| exam (competitive) | le concours |

| | |
|---|---|
| general education | **la culture générale** |
| instruction | **l'enseignement (m)** |
| *Language instruction is important.* | ***L'enseignement des langues est important.*** |
| knowledge | **les connaissances (fpl)** |
| lecture course | **le cours magistral** |
| master's degree | **la maîtrise** |
| Ph.D. | **le doctorat** |
| professor | **le professeur** |
| professorship | **la chaire** |
| registration | **l'inscription (f)** |
| rejected | **recalé(e)/rejeté(e)** |
| specialized education | **l'éducation (f)/la formation** |
| *Il a eu une excellente formation scientifique.* | ***He had an excellent scientific education.*** |
| university | **l'université (f)** |

## Higher Education Schools and Facilities

## Les écoles et les résidences universitaires

| | |
|---|---|
| School of Political Science | **la Faculté des Sciences Politiques** |
| School of Literature | **la Faculté des Lettres** |
| School of Law | **la Faculté de Droit** |
| School of Medicine | **la Faculté de Médecine** |
| School of Science and Technology | **la Faculté des Sciences et Techniques** |
| School of Arts | **la Faculté des Arts** |
| School of Fine Arts | **l'École des Beaux-Arts** |
| university cafeteria | **le restaurant universitaire** |
| university dorms/housing | **la cité universitaire** |
| *Many students enjoy living in university dorms.* | ***Beaucoup d'étudiants aiment bien la vie en cité universitaire.*** |
| language laboratory | **le laboratoire de langues** |
| research center | **le centre de recherches** |
| information center | **le centre de documentation** |

| | |
|---|---|
| library | la bibliothèque |
| student center | le centre d'étudiant |
| fitness center | le club fitness |
| weight training room | la salle de musculation |

## Distance Learning — L'enseignement à distance

| | |
|---|---|
| broadcast | la diffusion |
| course by correspondence | le cours par correspondance |
| distance professional development | la formation professionnelle à distance |
| fee/dues | la cotisation |
| forum | la plate-forme |
| interactive exercises | les exercices interactifs (mpl) |
| learning unit | le module |
| multimedia | le multimédia |
| night class | le cours du soir |
| online course | le cours en ligne |
| *I took online classes in accounting.* | *J'ai suivi des cours en ligne en comptabilité.* |
| online service | le service en ligne |
| subscribe | s'abonner/adhérer |
| subscriber | l'abonné(e)/l'adhérent(e) |
| subscription | l'abonnement |
| telecommunication | la télécommunication |
| virtual class | le cours virtuel |
| virtual conference | la conférence virtuelle |

## Professional Development — Les études professionnelles

| | |
|---|---|
| accounting | la comptabilité |
| architecture | l'architecture (f) |
| computer work | l'informatique (f) |
| construction | le bâtiment |
| *He is going to work in construction.* | *Il va travailler dans le bâtiment.* |
| cosmetology | les soins esthétiques (mpl) |

| | |
|---|---|
| fashion design | **la couture** |
| graphics | **le dessin** |
| landscaping | **le paysage** |
| management | **la gestion** |
| pharmaceuticals | **la pharmaceutique** |
| public work | **les travaux publics** |
| real estate | **l'immobilier (m)** |
| sales | **la vente** |
| surveying | **la topographie** |

# 5

# *Shopping*

# Buying, Selling, and Transactions

| | |
|---|---|
| bargain | **la bonne affaire** |
| bargain | **marchander** |
| cash register | **la caisse** |
| change | **la monnaie** |
| cheap | **bon marché** |
| *This one is cheaper than that one.* | ***Celui-ci est meilleur marché que celui-là.*** |
| cost | **coûter** |
| *How much does it cost?* | ***Ça coûte combien?*** |
| *How much is it?* | ***Ça fait combien?*** |
| credit | **le crédit** |
| *buy on credit* | ***acheter à crédit*** |
| credit card | **la carte de crédit** |
| discount | **le rabais/la réduction** |
| discount sales | **les soldes (fpl)** |
| excessively priced | **hors de prix** |
| expensive | **cher/chère** |
| free | **gratuit(e)** |
| money | **l'argent (m)** |
| on sale | **en réclame/en solde/en liquidation** |
| pay | **payer** |
| *pay cash* | ***payer en espèces*** |
| *pay in full* | ***payer comptant*** |
| payment | **le paiement** |
| price | **le prix** |
| purchase/buy | **acheter** |
| purchase | **l'achat (m)** |
| receipt | **le reçu** |
| retail | **au détail** |
| retailer | **le détaillant** |
| shop | **le magasin** |
| *shopping* | ***faire des achats*** |

| sale | la vente |
| *There is an auction sale today.* | *Il y a une vente aux enchères aujourd'hui.* |
| | |
| spend | dépenser |
| traveler's check | le chèque de voyage |
| wholesale | en gros |
| wholesaler | le vendeur/la vendeuse en gros |

## Customer Service

| closed | fermé(e) |
| *Closed on Sundays.* | *Fermé le dimanche.* |
| closing time | l'heure de fermeture (f) |
| customer | le/la client(e) |
| desire | désirer |
| dressing room | le salon d'essayage |
| elevator | l'ascenseur (m) |
| escalator | l'escalier roulant (m) |
| fire exit | la sortie de secours |
| help | aider |
| *Let me help you.* | *Permettez-moi de vous aider.* |
| help | l'aide (f) |
| merchandise | la marchandise |
| *No returns, no exchanges!* | *Pas de remboursement, pas d'échange!* |
| | |
| open | ouvrir |
| open | ouvert(e) |
| refund | le remboursement |
| salesperson | le vendeur/la vendeuse |
| security guard | le garde |
| sell | vendre |
| service desk | le service d'information |
| wrap | emballer |

# Stores

bookstore        **la librairie**

| | |
|---|---|
| boutique | **la boutique** |
| bridal shop | **la boutique de mariage** |
| consumer warehouse | **la grande surface** |
| department store | **le grand magasin** |
| flea market | **le marché aux puces** |
| flower shop | **chez le/la fleuriste** |
| *I go to the flower shop every Friday.* | *Je vais chez le fleuriste tous les vendredis.* |
| furniture store | **le magasin de meubles** |
| hardware store | **la quincaillerie** |
| jewelry shop | **la bijouterie** |
| leather goods store | **la maroquinerie** |
| mall | **le centre commercial** |
| market | **le marché** |
| newsstand | **le kiosque** |
| pawn shop | **le mont-de-piété** |
| pawnshop dealer | **le prêteur sur gages** |
| perfumery | **la parfumerie** |
| pharmacy | **la pharmacie** |
| *Get me some aspirin at the pharmacy.* | *Cherche-moi de l'aspirine à la pharmacie.* |
| shoe store | **le magasin de chaussures** |
| shopping center | **le centre commercial** |
| stationery store | **la papeterie** |

| supermarket | le supermarché/l'hypermarché |
| tobacco shop, tobacconist | le tabac/le bureau de tabac |
| upholstery shop | chez le tapissier |

# Food and Beverage

| ### Bakery | ### La boulangerie |
|---|---|
| bread | le pain |
| cake | le gâteau |
| cookie | le petit gâteau |
| cracker | le biscuit |
| croissant | le croissant |
| *I need a croissant with my coffee.* | *Il me faut un croissant avec mon café.* |
| pastry | la pâtisserie |
| roll | le petit pain |
| tart | la tarte |

| ### Butcher Shop | ### La boucherie |
|---|---|
| chicken | le poulet |
| cutlet | la côtelette |
| lamb | l'agneau (m) |
| leg of lamb | le gigot d'agneau |
| meat | la viande |
| pork | le porc |
| roast beef | le rosbif |
| steak | le bifteck/le steak |
| *Steak and french fries, please!* | *Un steak frites, s'il vous plaît!* |
| turkey | la dinde |
| veal | le veau |

| ### Deli | ### La charcuterie |
|---|---|
| ham | le jambon |
| pâté | le pâté |

| | |
|---|---|
| salad | la salade |
| salami | le salami |
| sandwich | le sandwich |
| sausage | la saucisse |
| turkey breast | de la dinde |

## Chocolate and Pastry Shops

## Les chocolateries et les pâtisseries

| | |
|---|---|
| cake | le gâteau |
| candy | les bonbons |
| *I eat a chocolate bar every day.* | *Je mange une tablette de chocolat chaque jour.* |
| chocolate shop | la chocolaterie |
| chocolate | le chocolat |
| confectioner's shop | la confiserie |
| pastry shop | la pâtisserie |
| sweets | les friandises/les sucreries (fpl) |
| tart | la tarte |

## Fish Market

## La poissonnerie

| | |
|---|---|
| clam | la palourde |
| cod | la morue |
| fish | le poisson |
| herring | le hareng |
| lobster | la langouste/le homard |
| mussel | la moule |
| *I cook mussels in white wine.* | *Je fais cuire les moules dans du vin blanc.* |
| oyster | l'huître (f) |
| salmon | le saumon |
| shell fish | les crustacés (mpl) |
| shrimp | la crevette |
| squid | le calmar |
| trout | la truite |

## Grocery Store

bay leaf
butter
cereal
coffee
condiments
egg(s)
*I use only fat-free milk.*
food
herbal tea
herbs
margarine
marmalade
mayonnaise
oil
olive oil
oregano
pepper
*Pass the pepper, please.*
salt
sauce
seasonings
shopping basket
shopping cart
shopping list
tea

## Fruit Market

fruit
grape
*Give me a bunch of grapes.*
melon
pineapple
raspberry

## L'épicerie

la feuille de laurier
le beurre
la céréale
le café
les condiments (mpl)
l'œuf/les œufs (m)
*Je n'utilise que le lait décrémé.*
les provisions (fpl)
la tisane
les herbes (fpl)
la margarine
la marmelade
la mayonnaise
l'huile (f)
l'huile d'olive (f)
l'origan (m)
le poivre
*Passe le poivre, s'il te plait.*
le sel
la sauce
les épices (fpl)
le panier
le chariot
la liste
le thé

## Le marché aux fruits

le fruit
le raisin
*Donnez-moi une grappe de raisin.*
le melon
l'ananas (m)
la framboise

| strawberry | **la fraise** |
| tomato | **la tomate** |
| watermelon | **la pastèque** |

## Vegetable Market     Le marché aux légumes

| artichoke | **l'artichaut (m)** |
| asparagus | **l'asperge (f)** |
| beet | **la betterave** |
| broccoli | **le brocoli** |
| brussel sprout | **le chou de Bruxelles** |
| cabbage | **le chou** |
| *Come here, honey!* | *Viens ici, mon chou!* |

 **Must-Know Tip**

Be aware that you are not being called a *cabbage* if someone addresses you as **mon chou**. It is a term of endearment like calling someone *honey*.

| carrot | **la carotte** |
| cauliflower | **le chou-fleur** |
| celery | **le céleri** |
| cucumber | **le concombre** |
| eggplant | **l'aubergine (f)** |
| green bean | **le haricot vert** |
| hot pepper | **le piment rouge** |
| leek | **le poireau** |
| lentil | **la lentille** |
| *I am making a lentil soup.* | *Je fais une soupe aux lentilles.* |
| lettuce | **la laitue** |
| onion | **l'oignon (m)** |
| pea | **le petit pois** |
| pepper | **le poivron** |
| potato | **la pomme de terre** |
| pumpkin | **la citrouille** |

| | |
|---|---|
| radish | **le radis** |
| spinach | **l'épinard** |
| squash | **la courge** |
| zucchini | **la courgette** |

# Clothes

| **Description** | **Description** |
|---|---|
| casual look | **le style décontracté** |
| checkered | **à carreaux** |
| cloth | **le tissu/l'étoffe (f)** |
| clothes | **les habits/les vêtements (mpl)** |
| clothing department | **le rayon des vêtements** |
| *Here is the ladies' department.* | *Voici le rayon des vêtements pour femmes.* |
| comfortable | **confortable** |
| corduroy | **le velours côtelé** |
| cotton | **le coton** |
| designer | **le grand couturier/la grande couturière** |
| elegant | **élégant(e)** |
| embroidered | **brodé(e)** |
| fashion | **la mode** |
| fashionable | **à la mode** |
| fit | **aller** |
| *Does it fit me?* | *Ça me va?* |
| hanger | **le cintre** |
| linen | **le lin** |
| long | **long/longue** |

| | |
|---|---|
| loose/wide | **large** |
| loud | **criard(e)** |
| man-made | **synthétique** |
| match | **assortir** |
| pleated | **plissé(e)** |
| polka dot | **à petits points** |
| print | **imprimé(e)** |
| sateen | **la satinette** |
| satin | **le satin** |
| short | **court(e)** |
| *Short skirts are back in fashion.* | *Les jupes courtes sont de nouveau à la mode.* |
| shrunk | **rétréci(e)** |
| silk | **la soie** |
| size | **la taille** |
| striped | **à rayures** |
| tight | **serré(e)** |
| velvet | **le velours** |
| wool | **la laine** |

## Garments

## Vêtements

**CASUAL**

**DE TOUS LES JOURS**

| | |
|---|---|
| apron | **le tablier** |
| blouse | **le chemisier** |
| blue jeans | **les jeans** |
| coat | **le manteau** |
| jacket | **la veste/le blouson** |
| *I want a leather jacket.* | *Je veux une veste en cuir.* |
| jogging suit | **le jogging** |
| overalls | **la salopette** |
| overcoat | **le pardessus** |
| pants | **le pantalon** |
| raincoat | **l'imperméable (m)** |
| scarf (winter) | **l'écharpe (f)** |

| scarf | le foulard/le fichu |
| shawl | le châle |
| *This green shawl fits you well.* | *Ce châle vert te va bien.* |
| shorts | le short |
| skirt | la jupe |
| sock | la chaussette |
| sweater | le pull(over) |
| sweatshirt | le sweat |
| swimsuit | le maillot (de bain) |
| T-shirt | le tee-shirt/le T-shirt |

## FORMAL AND PROFESSIONAL CLOTHES
## VÊTEMENTS DE SOIRÉE ET VÊTEMENTS PROFESSIONNELS

| bow tie | le nœud papillon |
| cuff (sleeve) | la manchette |
| dress code | la tenue vestimentaire |
| ensemble | l'ensemble (m) |
| *This skirt and vest ensemble looks good.* | *Cet ensemble jupe-veste est bien.* |
| evening gown | la robe de soirée |
| shirt (men's) | la chemise |
| shirt (women's) | le chemisier |
| suit (men's) | le costume |
| suit (women's) | le tailleur |
| tie | la cravate |
| tuxedo | le smoking |
| *Tuxedo required.* | *Smoking de rigueur.* |
| vest | le gilet |

## Undergarments and Nightclothes
## Les sous-vêtements et les vêtements de nuit

| brassiere | le soutien-gorge |
| brief | le caleçon |
| dressing gown | le peignoir |
| lingerie | la lingerie fine |

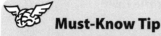

**Must-Know Tip**

Be aware that **la lingerie** can mean *linen* or *linen closet*. To avoid confusion, use **lingerie fine** or **lingerie pour dames** to talk about *lingerie*.

| | |
|---|---|
| nightgown | la chemise de nuit |
| pyjamas | le pyjama |
| robe | la robe de chambre |
| stockings | les bas (mpl) |
| *I buy only beige stockings.* | *Je n'achète que des bas beiges.* |
| tights | le collant |
| underpants/panties | la culotte |
| undershirt | la chemisette |
| underwear | le sous-vêtement |

## Shoes and Accessories

## Les chaussures et les accessoires

| | |
|---|---|
| bag | le sac |
| belt | la ceinture |
| boot | la botte |
| cap | la casquette |
| evening shoe | le soulier de bal |
| fancy leather goods | la maroquinerie |
| glove | le gant |
| high heel | le talon haut/talon aiguille |
| sandal | la sandale |
| *I need sandals for the beach.* | *J'ai besoin de sandales pour la plage.* |
| shoe size | la pointure |
| shoe store | le magasin de chaussures |
| shoelace | le lacet |
| slipper | la pantoufle |
| sneakers | les tennis/les baskets |

## Cleaning and Alterations

## Nettoyage et retouches

| | |
|---|---|
| alter | retoucher |
| button | le bouton |

| cleaners | la blanchisserie-teinturerie |
| dirty | sale |
| hem | l'ourlet (m) |
| *The hem must be altered.* | *Il faut retoucher l'ourlet.* |
| laundry | le linge |
| mend | raccommoder |
| patch | rapiécer |
| pin | l'épingle (f) |
| press/iron | repasser |
| saw | coudre |
| soiled | sale/taché(e) |
| spot/stain | la tache |
| torn | déchiré(e) |
| thread | le fil |
| try on | essayer |
| *Try the dress on!* | *Essaie la robe!* |
| wash | laver |
| wrinkled | froissé(e) |
| zipper | la fermeture-éclair/la tirette |

# Jewelry, Makeup, and Hair Products

## Jewelry                              ## Les bijoux

| bracelet | le bracelet |
| brooch | la broche |
| cuff links | les boutons de manchettes |
| *I have a pair of gold cuff links.* | *J'ai une paire de boutons de manchettes en or.* |
| diamond | le diamant |
| earring | la boucle d'oreille |
| emerald | l'émeraude (f) |
| jewel | le bijou |
| jewelry shop | la bijouterie |
| link chain | la chaîne |
| medallion | la médaille |

| necklace | le collier |
| pearl | la perle |
| pendant | le pendentif |
| ruby | le rubis |
| ring | la bague/l'anneau |
| *What a beautiful engagement ring!* | *Quelle belle bague de fiançailles!* |
| watch | la montre |
| wedding band | l'alliance (f) |

## Makeup — Produits de maquillage

| blush | le rouge |
| cosmetics | les produits de beauté |
| eyebrow pencil | le crayon à sourcils |
| eyeliner | le crayon yeux |
| eye shadow | le fard à paupières |
| face powder | la poudre |
| foundation makeup | la base |
| lipstick | le rouge à lèvres |
| mascara | le rimmel |
| tweezers | la pince à épiler |

## Hair Products — Produits pour les cheveux

| dye | teindre |
| *I dye my hair.* | *Je me teins les cheveux.* |
| hair color | la teinture capillaire |
| hair conditioner | le baume/le masque capillaire |
| hair relaxer | le produit défrisant |
| hair spray | la laque |
| perm | la permanente |
| styling gel | le gel coiffant |

# 6

# *A Place to Live*

# Housing

| Types of Housing and Characteristics | Les types d'habitation et leurs caractéristiques |
|---|---|
| air-conditioned | climatisé(e) |
| apartment building | l'immeuble (m) |
| apartment | l'appartement (m) |
| architecture | l'architecture (f) |
| building | le bâtiment |
| downtown | le centre-ville |
| duplex | le duplex |
| furnished | meublé(e) |
| house | la maison |
| *He is renting a furnished house.* | *Il loue une maison meublée.* |
| housing projects | les logements collectifs (mpl) |
| lodging | le logement |
| luxurious | de grand standing/luxueux(-se) |
| maintenance fees | les charges (fpl) |
| mortgage | l'hypothèque (f) |
| neighborhood | le quartier |
| noisy | bruyant(e) |
| plan | le plan |
| private | privé(e) |
| property | la propriété |
| quiet | tranquille |
| *She found a studio on a quiet block.* | *Elle a trouvé un studio dans une rue tranquille.* |
| renovated | rénové(e) |
| rent | le loyer |
| rent-controlled housing | l'habitation à loyer modéré (HLM) (f) |
| residence | le lieu de résidence/le lieu de domicile |

| | |
|---|---|
| residential development | **le complexe** |
| second floor | **le premier étage** |
| single family house | **le pavillon** |
| skyscraper | **le gratte-ciel** |
| space/room | **l'espace (m)** |
| spacious | **spacieux(-se)** |
| *Our office is spacious.* | *Notre bureau est spacieux.* |
| studio | **le studio** |
| suburb | **la banlieue** |
| sunny | **ensoleillé(e)** |
| tall building | **le building** |
| tower/multistory building | **la tour** |
| two room apartment | **le deux-pièces** |
| vacation/country house | **la villa** |
| vacation/second home | **la résidence secondaire** |
| *I have a second home in the country.* | *J'ai une résidence secondaire à la campagne.* |

## Layout and Rooms

## Plans et pièces

| | |
|---|---|
| attic | **le grenier** |
| balcony | **le balcon** |
| bathroom | **la salle de bains** |

 **Must-Know Tip**

Do not ask for a **salle de bains** in a public place; this term is reserved for a room including a bathtub or a shower. Ask for **les toilettes**.

| | |
|---|---|
| bedroom | **la chambre (à coucher)** |
| cellar | **la cave** |
| coded lock | **le digicode** |
| dining room | **la salle à manger** |

| | |
|---|---|
| door | **la porte** |
| elevator | **l'ascenseur (m)** |
| entrance | **l'entrée (f)** |
| *There is a bell at the entrance.* | *Il y a une sonnette à l'entrée.* |
| fireplace/chimney | **la cheminée** |
| first/ground floor | **le rez-de-chaussée** |
| floor/story | **l'étage (m)** |
| garage | **le garage** |
| garden | **le jardin** |
| guest room | **la chambre d'amis** |
| hallway | **le couloir/le hall** |
| intercom | **l'interphone** |
| *I speak to my friend on the inter-com before going in.* | *Je parle à mon ami à l'interphone avant de monter.* |
| kitchen | **la cuisine** |
| kitchenette | **la kitchenette** |
| living room | **le salon/la salle de séjour** |
| restroom | **le(s) cabinet(s)/le(s) W.C./les toilettes** |

 **Must-Know Tip**

In France, homes often have a restroom separate from the *bathroom* (the terms **cabinet(s)/W.C./toilettes** are all appropriate in this case). As mentioned previously, in a public place, the term for *restrooms* is **toilettes**.

| | |
|---|---|
| roof | **le toit** |
| stairs | **l'escalier (m)** |
| step | **la marche** |
| terrace | **la terrasse** |
| window | **la fenêtre** |
| yard | **la cour** |
| *There is an inside yard.* | *Il y a une cour intérieure.* |

# Buying, Renting, and Selling

| | |
|---|---|
| borrow | **emprunter** |
| broker | **le courtier** |
| buy | **acheter** |
| co-owner | **le/la copropriétaire** |
| deed | **l'acte de vente (m)** |
| down payment | **l'acompte (m)/les arrhes (fpl)** |
| *house for sale* | *maison à vendre* |
| *house sold* | *maison vendue* |
| in escrow | **en séquestre** |
| interest rate | **le taux d'intérêt** |
| *The interest rate is advantageous.* | *Le taux d'intérêt est avantageux.* |
| landlord/owner | **le/la propriétaire** |
| lease | **le bail/le contrat** |
| lease purchase | **l'achat de bail (m)** |
| lend | **prêter/faire un prêt** |
| loan | **le prêt** |
| mortgage | **l'hypothèque (f)** |
| real estate agency | **l'agence immobilière (f)** |
| real estate agent | **l'agent immobilier (m)** |
| real estate | **l'immobilier (m)** |
| rent | **le loyer** |
| *My rent is going up.* | *Mon loyer va augmenter.* |
| rent | **louer** |
| sublease | **sous-louer** |
| sales commission | **la commission** |
| security deposit | **la garantie/le cautionnement** |
| sell | **vendre** |
| tenant | **le/la locataire** |

# Furniture, Accessories, and Household Appliances

| Furniture and Accessories | Meubles et accessoires |
|---|---|
| armchair | le fauteuil |
| armoire/wardrobe | l'armoire (f) |
| bathroom sink | le lavabo |
| *What a pretty mirror above the sink!* | *Quel joli miroir au-dessus du lavabo!* |
| bathtub | la baignoire |
| bed | le lit |
| bedspread | le couvre-lit |
| bolster | le traversin |
| chair | la chaise |
| chandelier | le lustre/le chandelier |
| chest of drawers/dresser | la commode |
| closet | le placard |
| comforter | l'édredon (m)/la couette |
| couch | le divan/le canapé |
| *You need cushions on this couch.* | *Tu as besoin de coussins sur ce divan.* |
| curtain | le rideau |
| desk | le bureau |
| double bed | le grand lit |
| kitchen sink | l'évier (m) |
| knickknack | le bibelot |
| lamp | la lampe |
| mirror | la glace/le miroir |
| nightstand | la table de chevet |
| picture/painting | le tableau |
| piece of furniture | le meuble |
| *I need new furniture.* | *Il me faut de nouveaux meubles.* |
| pillow | l'oreiller (m) |
| rug | le tapis |
| shade | le store |
| sheet | le drap |

| shelves | l'étagère (f) |
| shutter | le volet |
| sofa | le sofa |
| stereo system | la chaîne stéréo |
| table | la table |
| throw pillow | le coussin |
| vase | le vase |
| wallpaper | le papier peint |
| wall-to-wall carpet | la moquette |

## Household Appliances — Les appareils ménagers

| blender | le mixeur |
| burner | la plaque de cuisson |
| dishwasher | le lave-vaisselle |
| *I use my dishwasher regularly.* | *Je me sers de mon lave-vaisselle régulièrement.* |
| dryer | le sèche-linge |
| fan | le ventilateur |
| food processor | le robot cuisine |
| freezer | le congélateur |
| garbage disposal | le vide-ordures |
| hair dryer | le sèche-cheveux |
| iron | le fer à repasser |
| microwave oven | le (four à) micro-ondes |
| oven | le four |
| radiator | le radiateur |
| *The radiator does not work.* | *Le radiateur ne marche pas.* |
| refrigerator/fridge | le réfrigérateur/le frigo |
| stove | la cuisinière |
| toaster | le grille-pain |
| vacuum cleaner | l'aspirateur (m) |
| washing machine | la machine à laver |
| water heater | le chauffe-eau |

# Housework and Daily Routines

## Household Chores

clean house
clean the floors
clear the table
cook
*I never cook.*
dust the furniture
dustpan
empty the garbage can
housekeeper
iron
make the bed
scrub
set the table
sweep
take out the trash
tidy up
*Tidy up your room!*
vacuum
ventilate
warm/heat
wash the dishes
wash the laundry
wash the windows
water the plants
wax the wooden floor
wipe/dry
*Those glasses need to be wiped dry.*

## Les tâches ménagères

**faire le ménage**
**nettoyer le carrelage**
**débarrasser la table**
**faire la cuisine**
*Je ne fais jamais la cuisine.*
**épousseter/faire la poussière**
**la pelle**
**vider la poubelle**
**la femme de ménage**
**repasser**
**faire le lit**
**frotter**
**mettre la table**
**balayer/donner un coup de balai**
**sortir les ordures**
**ranger/organiser/mettre de l'ordre**
*Range ta chambre!*
**passer l'aspirateur**
**aérer**
**chauffer/réchauffer**
**laver la vaisselle**
**faire la lessive/laver le linge**
**laver les fenêtres**
**arroser les plantes**
**cirer le parquet**
**essuyer**
*Il faut essuyer ces verres.*

## Daily Routines

answer messages
brush teeth

## Les activités quotidiennes

**répondre aux messages**
**se brosser les dents**

| | |
|---|---|
| change | **se changer** |
| chat | **bavarder** |
| dance | **danser** |
| discuss | **discuter** |
| do homework | **faire les devoirs** |
| dream | **rêver** |
| dress | **s'habiller** |
| drive | **conduire** |
| eat breakfast | **prendre le petit déjeuner** |
| eat dinner | **dîner** |
| eat lunch | **déjeuner** |
| fall asleep | **s'endormir** |
| *I fall asleep dreaming.* | *Je m'endors en rêvant.* |
| feed the cat | **donner à manger au chat** |
| get up | **se lever** |
| go home | **rentrer à la maison** |
| go to an evening party | **aller à une soirée** |
| go to bed | **se coucher** |
| go to school | **aller à l'école/au cours** |
| go to the disco/nightclub | **aller en boîte** |
| *Young people go to discos.* | *Les jeunes vont en boîte.* |
| go to the gym | **aller au gymnase** |
| go to work | **aller au travail** |
| groom oneself | **faire sa toilette** |
| have a coffee/soda | **boire un café/soda** |
| have a snack | **prendre un goûter** |
| have fun | **s'amuser** |
| hurry | **se dépêcher** |
| listen to music | **écouter de la musique** |
| make phone calls | **téléphoner/passer des coups de fil** |
| meet friends | **rencontrer/retrouver des amis** |
| *Je retrouve mes amis au café.* | *I meet my friends at the café.* |
| prepare dinner | **préparer le dîner** |
| read the paper | **lire le journal** |

| rest | **se reposer** |
| shave | **se raser** |
| sleep | **dormir** |
| study | **étudier** |
| take a shower | **prendre une douche** |
| take the bus/subway | **prendre le bus/le métro** |
| wake up | **se réveiller** |
| walk the dog | **promener/sortir le chien** |
| walk (going on foot) | **marcher/aller à pied** |
| walk/stretch one's legs (taking a walk) | **faire une balade/faire une promenade** |
| *I walk to the office to stretch my legs.* | *Je marche jusqu'au bureau pour faire une petite balade.* |

 **Must-Know Tip**

Be aware that the noun **la marche** is most often used to mean *a march* in the military sense. It can also be a well-planned walk as in hiking.

| wash | **se laver** |
| watch TV | **regarder la télé** |

# 7

# *At Work*

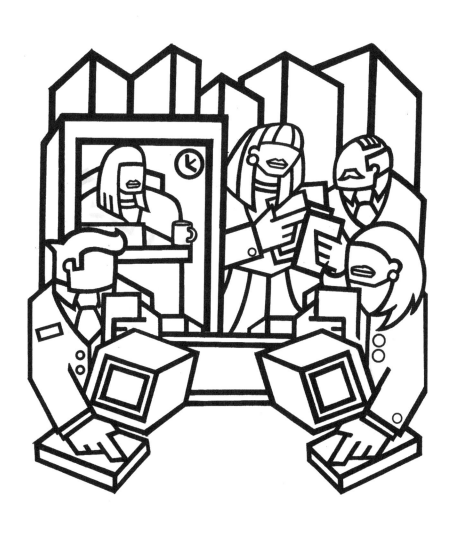

# Career Choices and Training

## Trades and Skills

baker
butcher
clock/watchmaker
cosmetologist
hairdresser
jeweler
mechanic
*The mechanic repairs motorcycles.*
pastry chef
photographer
salesperson
seamstress
shoemaker
tailor
tradesperson

## Le commerce et les métiers

**le boulanger/la boulangère**
**le boucher/la bouchère**
**l'horloger/l'horlogère**
**l'esthéticien(ne)**
**le coiffeur/la coiffeuse**
**le joailler/la joaillère**
**le/la mécanicien(ne); le/la garagiste**
*Le mécanicien répare les motos.*
**le pâtissier/la pâtissière**
**le/la photographe**
**le vendeur/la vendeuse**
**la couturière**
**le cordonnier/la cordonnière**
**le tailleur**
**le/la commerçant(e)**

## Construction and Home Repairs

apprentice
architect
*The architect has an intern.*
carpenter
construction worker
contractor
craftsman
electrician
engineer
gardener
mason
painter
plumber

## La construction et les réparations

**l'apprenti(e)**
**l'architecte**
*L'architecte a un stagiaire.*
**le menuisier**
**l'ouvrier/l'ouvrière**
**l'entrepreneur/l'entrepreneuse**
**l'artisan (m)**
**l'électricien(ne)**
**l'ingénieur (m)**
**le jardinier/la jardinière**
**le maçon**
**le/la peintre**
**le plombier**

| | |
|---|---|
| roofer | le couvreur |
| tile layer | le carreleur |

## Tourism

## Le tourisme

| | |
|---|---|
| chef | **le chef** |
| cook | **le cuisinier/la cuisinière** |
| driver (car/truck) | **le chauffeur** |
| *The cab driver receives many tips.* | *Le chauffeur de taxi reçoit beaucoup de pourboires.* |
| bus driver | **le conducteur/la conductrice d'autobus** |
| tow truck driver | **le dépanneur** |

### Must-Know Tip

Be aware that the term **dépanneur** varies in Québec where it means *grocery store.*

| | |
|---|---|
| flight attendant | **le steward/l'hôtesse de l'air (f)** |
| guide | **le/la guide** |
| pilot | **le pilote** |
| travel agent | **l'agent de voyage (m)** |
| waiter, waitress/server | **le serveur/la serveuse** |

## Career Training

## Préparation à une carrière

| | |
|---|---|
| apply for | **postuler/poser sa candidature** |
| executive | **le cadre** |
| *He is a top executive.* | *C'est un cadre supérieur.* |
| get a promotion | **obtenir une promotion** |
| internship | **le stage** |
| job opening | **le débouché** |
| make a career | **faire carrière** |
| occupation | **l'emploi (m)/l'occupation (f)** |

| | |
|---|---|
| practice | le cabinet |
| qualified | qualifié(e) |
| résumé | le CV/curriculum vitae |
| retrain | se recycler |
| specialization | la spécialisation |
| specialize | se spécialiser |
| train | former |
| training | la formation |
| *His training is in computer science.* | *Sa formation est dans l'informatique.* |
| worker | le travailleur/la travailleuse;<br>l'ouvrier/l'ouvrière; le/la salarié(e) |

# Workplace, Equipment, and Tools

## At the Office

## Au bureau

| | |
|---|---|
| ballpoint pen | le stylo |
| calculator | la calculette/calculatrice |
| calendar | le calendrier |
| computer | l'ordinateur (m) |
| desk | le bureau |
| dictaphone | le dictaphone |
| fax machine | la télécopieuse |
| fax | le fax/la télécopie |
| fax | faxer/télécopier |
| file | le dossier |
| *Where is my medical file?* | *Où est mon dossier médical?* |
| filing cabinet | le classeur |
| filing case | le fichier |
| folder/cover | la chemise |
| highlighter | le marqueur/surligneur |
| hole punch | la perforatrice |
| ink cartridge | la cartouche d'encre |
| letterhead | l'en-tête (m) |

| notepad | le bloc-notes |
|---|---|
| office | le bureau |
| paper clip | le trombone |
| photocopier | la photocopieuse |
| *The photocopier is down.* | *La photocopieuse ne marche plus.* |
| printer | l'imprimante (f) |
| recycled paper | le papier recyclé |
| scanner | le scanneur/le scanner |
| sheet (of paper) | la feuille |
| staple | l'agrafe (f) |
| stapler | l'agrafeuse (f) |
| sort/file | classer |
| typewriter | la machine à écrire |
| wastebasket | le panier |
| word processor | le logiciel/traitement de texte |

## At the Bank / À la banque

| ATM | le distributeur automatique |
|---|---|
| bank | la banque |
| branch | la succursale |
| *My bank opened a new branch.* | *Ma banque a ouvert une nouvelle succursale.* |
| checkbook | le chéquier/le carnet de chèques |
| PIN | le code secret |
| safe/safe deposit box | le coffre-fort |
| savings bank | la caisse d'épargne |
| teller's window | la caisse/le guichet |
| vault | la chambre forte |

## Landscaping / Le jardinage

| fertilizer | l'engrais (m) |
|---|---|
| hose | le tuyau |
| ladder | l'échelle (f) |
| lawn mower | la tondeuse |

| | |
|---|---|
| measuring tape | **le mètre** |
| rake | **le rateau** |
| rake | **ratisser** |
| *We'd better rake all those dead leaves.* | ***Il vaudrait mieux ratisser toutes ces feuilles mortes.*** |
| scissors | **les ciseaux (mpl)** |
| shovel | **la pelle** |
| sprinkler | **l'arroseuse (f) à jet tournant/le tourniquet** |

## Construction

## La construction

| | |
|---|---|
| brick | **la brique** |
| bulldozer | **le bulldozer** |
| chisel | **le burin** |
| concrete mixer | **la bétonnière** |
| crane | **la grue** |
| drill | **la perceuse électrique** |
| file | **la lime** |
| hammer | **le marteau** |
| *He hit the nail with the hammer.* | ***Il a enfoncé le clou avec le marteau.*** |
| ladder | **l'échelle (f)** |
| machine | **la machine** |
| nail | **le clou** |
| pick | **le pic** |
| pliers | **la pince** |
| saw | **la scie** |
| scaffolding | **l'échafaudage (m)** |
| screw | **la vis** |
| screwdriver | **le tourne-vis** |
| tool | **l'outil (m)** |
| *The carpenter can't do anything without his tools.* | ***Le menuisier ne peut rien faire sans ses outils.*** |
| wrench | **la clé** |

# Working Conditions

## Looking for a Job

apply (for a job)
classified ads
contract
employment agency
find
hire
job

job application
*She is filling out a job application.*

jobs wanted
look for
place a person
vacancy

## Job Performance

agenda
appoint
appointment
company
*I work for a real estate company.*

employee
employer
laborer
personnel
promotion
work
*work full time*

## La recherche d'un emploi

**postuler/poser sa candidature**
**les petites annonces (fpl)**
**le contrat**
**un bureau de placement**
**trouver**
**embaucher/engager**
**l'emploi (m)/le travail/le job/le boulot**
**le formulaire de candidature**
*Elle remplit un formulaire de candidature.*

**les demandes d'emploi (fpl)**
**chercher**
**placer une personne**
**l'offre d'emploi (f)**

## La performance

**l'agenda/l'ordre du jour (m)**
**nommer**
**le rendez-vous**
**la société/l'entreprise**
*Je travaille pour une société immobilière.*

**l'employé(e)**
**le patron/la patronne**
**l'ouvrier/l'ouvrière**
**le personnel**
**la promotion**
**le travail**
*travailler à plein temps*

| | |
|---|---|
| *work part time* | *travailler à temps partiel* |
| *work at home* | *travailler à domicile* |
| worker | **le travailleur/la travailleuse** |

## Compensation and Benefits — Rémunération et avantages

| | |
|---|---|
| advance | **l'avance (f)** |
| bonus | **la prime** |
| daily wage | **le salaire journalier** |
| days off | **les jours libres/congés (mpl)** |
| earn | **gagner** |
| fringe benefits | **les prestations sociales (fpl)** |
| holiday | **le jour férié** |
| minimum wage | **le salaire minimum/le SMIC** |
| *These employees earn the minimum wage.* | *Ces employés gagnent le SMIC.* |
| pay raise | **l'augmentation (f)** |
| payday | **le jour de paie** |
| pension | **la pension** |
| remuneration | **la rémunération** |
| retirement | **la retraite** |
| salary/wages | **le salaire/le traitement** |
| sick leave | **les congés maladie (mpl)** |
| Social Security | **la Sécurité Sociale** |
| take a long weekend | **faire le pont** |
| vacation | **les vacances (fpl)/les congés (mpl)** |
| *This firm gives three weeks of paid vacation.* | *Cette société donne trois semaines de congés payés.* |

## Unemployment and Workers' Rights — Le chômage et les droits du travailleur

| | |
|---|---|
| agreement | **l'accord (m)** |
| association | **l'association (f)** |
| boss | **le patron/la patronne** |
| boycott | **le boycott** |

| | |
|---|---|
| boycott | **boycotter** |
| collective wage agreement | **la convention collective** |
| compromise | **le compromis** |
| *We must reach a compromise.* | *Il faut trouver un compromis.* |
| contribution | **la cotisation** |
| demand | **la revendication** |
| demand | **revendiquer/exiger** |

 **Must-Know Tip**

Be aware that the French word **demander** means nothing more than *to ask*. It is a false cognate. *To demand* is **exiger**.

| | |
|---|---|
| dismissal; layoff | **le licenciement/le renvoi** |
| employers and employees | **les partenaires sociaux** |
| form a union | **se syndiquer** |
| go back to work | **reprendre le travail** |
| labor dispute | **le conflit social** |
| layoff | **congédier/licencier** |
| lockout | **le lockout** |
| mediator | **le médiateur/la médiatrice** |
| negotiate | **négocier** |
| negotiation | **la négociation** |
| *Negotiations are going well.* | *Les négociations se poursuivent bien.* |
| oppose/fight | **militer/lutter/combattre** |
| protest/demonstration | **la manifestation** |
| protest | **manifester/contester** |
| resign | **démissionner** |
| resignation | **la démission** |
| severance pay | **l'indemnité (f)** |
| solution | **la solution** |
| strike | **la grève** |
| *Teachers are on strike.* | *Les enseignants font la grève.* |

| | |
|---|---|
| *solidarity strike* | *la grève de solidarité* |
| striker | **le/la gréviste** |
| unemployed | **le chômeur/la chômeuse** |
| unemployment | **le chômage** |
| *unemployment benefits* | *les allocations chômage* |
| union | **le syndicat** |
| wage earner | **le/la salarié(e)** |
| walk out | **débrayer** |

# Finance, Business, and the Economy

## Finance

## Les finances

| | |
|---|---|
| account balance | **le solde** |
| account | **le compte** |
| bank account | **le compte en banque** |
| credit | **le crédit** |
| currency | **la monnaie** |
| deposit | **le versement** |
| *This is my last deposit this month.* | *C'est mon dernier versement ce mois-ci.* |
| deposit | **verser** |
| exchange | **échanger** |
| interest rate | **le taux d'intérêt** |
| interest | **les intérêts (mpl)** |
| investment | **le placement** |
| loan | **le prêt** |
| money transfer | **le transfert** |
| password | **le mot de passe** |
| PIN | **le code secret** |
| rate of exchange | **le taux d'échange** |
| save (money) | **économiser/épargner** |
| savings account | **le compte d'épargne** |
| *Open a savings account and save!* | *Ouvre un compte d'épargne et économise!* |

| | |
|---|---|
| savings and loan association | **la caisse d'épargne** |
| statement | **le bilan** |
| withdraw | **débiter** |
| withdrawal | **le débit** |

## Business / Les affaires

| | |
|---|---|
| bankruptcy | **la banqueroute/la faillite** |
| bill | **la facture** |
| budget | **le budget** |
| chamber of commerce | **la chambre de commerce** |
| cash register | **la caisse** |
| cash | **les espèces (fpl)/l'argent liquide (m)** |
| *I do not have cash.* | *Je n'ai pas d'argent liquide.* |
| collateral | **la garantie** |
| company | **la société/l'entreprise (f)** |
| competition | **la concurrence** |
| corporation | **la Société Anonyme/la SA** |
| general manager | **le PDG (président-directeur-général)** |
| income tax | **les impôts (sur le revenu) (mpl)** |
| income tax return | **la déclaration de revenu** |
| income tax agency | **le fisc** |
| insurance company | **la société d'assurances** |
| invoice | **la facture** |
| liability | **la responsabilité légale** |
| management | **la direction** |
| nonprofit | **à but non lucratif** |
| *She works for a nonprofit organization.* | *Elle travaille pour une société à but non lucratif.* |
| partner | **l'associé(e)** |
| sales tax | **la taxe sur la valeur ajoutée/TVA** |
| tax-exempt | **exempt de taxe** |

## The Economy

| | **L'économie** |
|---|---|
| assets | **le capital** |
| auction | **la vente aux enchères** |
| balance of trade | **la balance du commerce** |
| cost of living | **le coût de la vie** |
| debt | **la dette** |
| downward move | **la baisse** |
| economic recovery | **le redressement économique** |
| gain | **les revenus (mpl)** |
| inflation | **l'inflation (f)** |
| *Prices rise with inflation.* | ***Les prix montent avec l'inflation.*** |
| investment | **l'investissement (m)/le placement** |
| investor | **l'investisseur (m)** |
| loss | **la perte** |
| profit | **le profit/le bénéfice** |
| quote | **coter** |
| recession; slump | **la récession** |
| share | **l'action (f)** |
| shareholder | **l'actionnaire (m/f)** |
| speculator/trader | **le spéculateur/la spéculatrice** |
| stock exchange; market | **la bourse** |
| *The stock exchange goes up and down.* | ***La bourse a des hauts et des bas.*** |
| supply and demand | **l'offre (f) et la demande** |
| supply | **fournir** |
| takeover | **l'acquisition (f)** |
| upward move | **la hausse** |

# 8

# *Leisure Time*

# Arts and Multimedia

## Cinema and Theater

## Le cinéma et le théâtre

| | |
|---|---|
| act | l'acte (m) |
| act | jouer |
| actor | l'acteur/le comédien |
| actress | l'actrice/la comédienne |
| applaud, clap | applaudir |
| applause | l'applaudissement (m) |
| audience | le public/l'assistance |
| award | le prix |
| climax | l'apogée (f) |
| comedian | le/la comique |
| critic | le/la critique |
| *I do not share this critic's opinion.* | *Je ne partage pas l'opinion de ce critique.* |
| curtain | le rideau |
| dubbed | doublé |
| ending | la fin |
| exciting | excitant(e)/passionnant(e) |
| film | tourner un film |
| flop | le navet |
| funny | drôle/comique |
| hiss | siffler |
| movie star | la vedette de cinéma |
| movie | le film |
| movie fan | le/la cinéphile |
| moving | émouvant(e) |
| *The departure scene is very moving.* | *La scène du départ est émouvante.* |
| play | la pièce |
| playwright | le/la dramaturge |
| plot | l'action (f)/le déroulement |

| | |
|---|---|
| premiere | **la première** |
| rehearsal | **la répétition** |
| rehearse | **répéter** |
| role | **le rôle** |
| seat | **la place** |
| scene | **la scène** |
| screen | **l'écran (m)** |
| *Movie fans love the big screen.* | ***Les cinéphiles adorent le grand écran.*** |
| script | **le script** |
| show | **le spectacle/la représentation** |
| stage | **la scène** |
| stage fright | **le trac** |
| success | **le succès** |
| tragic | **tragique** |

## Music and Dance

## La musique et la danse

### GENERAL TERMS

### GÉNÉRALITÉS

| | |
|---|---|
| applause | **les applaudissements (mpl)** |
| concert hall | **la salle de concert** |
| concert | **le concert** |
| *I like outdoor concerts.* | ***J'aime les concerts en plein air.*** |
| musical comedy | **l'opérette (f)/la comédie musicale** |
| musician | **le musicien/la musicienne** |
| open dance | **le bal public** |
| opera | **l'opéra (m)** |
| orchestra | **l'orchestre (m)** |
| gala | **le gala** |
| recital | **le récital** |
| recording | **l'enregistrement (m)** |
| seat | **la place** |
| show | **le spectacle/la représentation** |

| | |
|---|---|
| *The show is about to start.* | *Le spectacle va commencer.* |
| sound system | **la sonorisation** |
| ticket | **le billet** |
| tour | **la tournée** |
| virtuoso | **le/la virtuose** |

## TYPES OF MUSIC — LES TYPES DE MUSIQUE

| | |
|---|---|
| classical music | **la musique classique** |
| country music | **la musique country** |
| jazz | **le jazz** |
| pop music | **la musique pop** |
| rap music | **la musique rap** |
| *I like rap music very much.* | *La musique rap me plaît beaucoup.* |
| reggae music | **le reggae** |
| rock | **le rock** |
| sonata | **la sonate** |
| symphony | **la symphonie** |

## MUSICAL INSTRUMENTS — LES INSTRUMENTS DE MUSIQUE

| | |
|---|---|
| accordion | **l'accordéon (m)** |
| acoustic guitar | **la guitare acoustique** |
| amplifier | **l'amplificateur (m)** |
| banjo | **le banjo** |
| cello | **le violoncelle** |
| clarinet | **la clarinette** |
| drum | **le tambour** |
| drums | **la batterie** |
| electric guitar | **la guitare électrique** |
| *He plays the electric guitar.* | *Il joue de la guitare électrique.* |
| electronic keyboard | **l'orgue électronique (m)** |
| flute | **la flûte** |
| French horn | **le cor d'harmonie** |
| harmonica | **l'harmonica (m)** |
| harp | **la harpe** |
| mandolin | **la mandoline** |

| organ | l'orgue (m) |
| piano | le piano |
| saxophone | le saxophone |
| trumpet | la trompette |
| violin | le violon |
| *He learns to play the violin.* | *Il apprend à jouer du violon.* |

 **Must-Know Tip**

Remember to use **de la**, **de l'**, or **du** before an instrument one plays (Je joue **du violon**). However, use **à la**, **à l'**, or **au** before a sport or a game one plays (Je joue **au tennis**).

### TYPES OF DANCING
ballet
ballroom dancing
classical dance
folk dancing
modern dance
tap dancing

### LES TYPES DE DANSE
**le ballet**
**la danse traditionnelle**
**la danse classique**
**la danse folklorique**
**la danse moderne**
**les claquettes**

## Fine Arts

## Les beaux-arts

### GENERAL TERMS
art
art gallery
artist
exhibition
*There is a Picasso exhibit at the museum.*
fine arts
graphic arts
masterpiece

### GÉNÉRALITÉS
**l'art (m)**
**la galerie d'art**
**l'artiste (m/f)**
**l'exposition (f)**
*Il y a une exposition Picasso au musée.*
**les beaux-arts (mpl)**
**les arts graphiques (mpl)**
**le chef-d'œuvre**

| | |
|---|---|
| visual arts | **les arts plastiques (mpl)** |
| work of art | **l'œuvre d'art (f)** |

## PAINTING — LA PEINTURE

| | |
|---|---|
| brush | **le pinceau** |
| canvas | **la toile** |
| impressionism | **l'impressionnisme (m)** |
| modern art | **l'art moderne (m)** |
| oil painting | **la peinture à l'huile** |
| paint | **peindre** |
| palette | **la palette** |
| picture/painting | **le tableau** |
| *This is an original painting.* | ***C'est un tableau original.*** |
| portrait | **le portrait** |
| studio | **l'atelier (m)** |
| watercolor | **l'aquarelle (f)** |

## POTTERY, SCULPTURE, AND CERAMICS — LA POTERIE, LA SCULPTURE ET LA CÉRAMIQUE

| | |
|---|---|
| bronze | **le bronze** |
| bust | **le buste** |
| ceramics | **la céramique** |
| clay | **l'argile (f)** |
| life-size | **grandeur nature** |
| *Rodin sculpted many life-size statues.* | ***Rodin a sculpté beaucoup de statues grandeur nature.*** |
| marble | **le marbre** |
| miniature | **la miniature** |
| model | **le modèle** |
| pottery | **la poterie** |
| print/engraving | **la gravure** |
| sculpt | **sculpter** |
| sculpture | **la sculpture** |
| statue | **la statue** |

| ARCHITECTURE | L'ARCHITECTURE |
|---|---|
| baroque | baroque |
| classical | classique |
| *The palace of Versailles is an example of classical architecture.* | *Le château de Versailles est un exemple d'architecture classique.* |
| contemporary | contemporain(e) |
| Gothic | gothique |
| romanesque | roman(e) |
| urban | urbain(e) |

## Television and Radio — La télévision et la radio

| advertising | la publicité |
|---|---|
| announcer | le présentateur/la présentatrice |
| band | le groupe |
| broadcast | retransmettre/diffuser |
| broadcast/show | l'émission (f) |
| cable TV | la télévision par câble |
| cartoon | le dessin animé |
| *Pépé le Pew is my favorite cartoon.* | *Pépé le Pew est mon dessin animé favori.* |
| character | le personnage |
| comedy | la comédie |
| detective/police movie | le film policier |
| encoded channel | la chaîne codée |
| game show | le jeu télévisé |
| guest | l'invité(e) |
| listener | l'auditeur/l'auditrice |
| listeners | le public/l'audience |
| listening | à l'écoute |
| live broadcast | l'émission en direct (f) |
| moderator | l'animateur/l'animatrice |
| movie/TV star | la vedette |
| *He is the star of the series.* | *C'est lui, la vedette de la série.* |

| | |
|---|---|
| news | **les actualités/les informations (fpl)** |
| private station | **la chaîne privée** |
| public station | **la chaîne publique** |
| radio | **la radio** |
| receive | **capter** |
| report | **faire un reportage** |
| report | **le reportage** |
| satellite TV | **la télévision par satellite** |
| science-fiction movie | **le film de science-fiction** |
| short film | **le court-métrage** |
| *This short film won a prize at the Cannes festival.* | *Ce court-métrage a gagné un prix au festival de Cannes.* |
| singer | **le chanteur/la chanteuse** |
| soap opera | **le feuilleton** |
| song | **la chanson** |
| suspense movie | **le film de suspense** |
| talk show | **le talk show** |
| television program | **le programme/l'émission (f)** |
| TV movie | **le téléfilm** |
| TV news program | **le journal télévisé** |
| TV series | **la série télévisée/le feuilleton** |
| variety show | **les variétés (fpl)** |
| waves (long/short/medium) | **les ondes (grandes/petites/ moyennes)** |
| western movie | **le western** |
| with time delay | **en différé** |

## Computers

## Les ordinateurs

| | |
|---|---|
| antivirus program | **le programme anti-virus** |
| *An antivirus program protects my computer from hackers.* | *Un programme anti-virus protège mon ordinateur des pirates.* |
| browser | **l'explorateur (m)** |
| CD-ROM drive | **le lecteur de CD-ROM** |
| CD-ROM | **le CD-ROM/le cédérom** |

| | |
|---|---|
| chat | **chatter** |
| click | **cliquer** |
| computer game | **le jeu vidéo** |
| computer specialist | **l'informaticien(ne)** |
| crash | **se bloquer** |
| cursor | **le curseur** |
| disk drive | **le lecteur de disquette** |
| electronic game | **le jeu électronique** |
| electronic mailbox | **la boîte aux lettres électronique** |
| e-mail | **le mél/e-mail/courriel** |
| *I send e-mails every day.* | ***J'envoie des courriels tous les jours.*** |
| floppy disk | **la disquette** |
| free access | **accès gratuit** |
| hacker | **le pirate** |
| hard disk | **le disque dur** |
| hardware | **le matériel** |
| home page | **la page d'accueil** |
| information superhighway | **l'autoroute de l'information (f)** |
| ink-jet printer | **l'imprimante à jet d'encre (f)** |
| install | **installer** |
| Internet | **Internet/le Net** |
| Internet café | **le cybercafé** |
| *Abroad, I look for Internet cafés.* | ***À l'étranger je cherche des cybercafés.*** |
| laptop | **le portable** |
| laser printer | **l'imprimante à laser (f)** |
| load/start | **charger/démarrer** |
| log on | **se connecter** |
| monitor | **le moniteur/l'écran (m)** |
| mouse | **la souris** |
| password | **le mot de passe** |
| personal computer | **le PC** |
| play station | **la console de jeux vidéo** |
| print | **imprimer** |
| *Print the instructions!* | ***Imprime les instructions!*** |

| | |
|---|---|
| *right to log in* | *le droit d'accès* |
| *search engine* | *le moteur de recherche* |
| software | **le logiciel** |
| type | **taper** |
| user | **l'utilisateur/l'utilisatrice;** |
| | **l'usager/l'usagère** |
| video games | **les jeux vidéo** |
| website | **le site web** |
| word processing program | **le traitement de texte** |

# Reading

## Literature

## La littérature

| | |
|---|---|
| adventure novel | **le roman d'aventure** |
| author | **l'auteur(e)** |
| biography | **la biographie** |
| conference/lecture | **la conférence** |
| *I attend lectures on my favorite poets.* | *Je vais à des conférences sur mes poètes favoris.* |
| detective novel | **le roman policier** |
| fiction | **la fiction** |
| historical novel | **le roman historique** |
| horror novel | **le roman noir** |
| illustration | **l'illustration (f)** |
| lecture | **le cours/la conférence** |
| lecturer | **le conférencier/la conférencière** |
| literary era | **l'époque littéraire (f)** |
| literary movement | **le mouvement littéraire** |
| literary work | **l'œuvre (littéraire) (f)** |
| *Camus's literary works are known.* | *Les œuvres de Camus sont connues.* |
| novelist | **le romancier/la romancière** |
| number/issue | **l'album (m)** |

| | |
|---|---|
| plot | l'intrigue (f) |
| poem | le poème |
| poet | le poète/la poétesse |
| poetry | la poésie |
| science-fiction novel | le roman de science fiction |
| script | le scénario |
| *study of languages and literature* | *les lettres (fpl)* |
| writer | l'écrivain(e) |
| *Anne Hébert is a writer from Québec.* | *Anne Hébert est une écrivaine québécoise.* |

## Magazines and Publications

## Les magazines et les publications

| | |
|---|---|
| ad | la petite annonce |
| article | l'article (m) |
| bubble | la bulle |
| caricature | le dessin humoristique/la caricature |
| cartoonist | le dessinateur/la dessinatrice |
| column | la rubrique |
| comic strip | la bande dessinée |
| crossword puzzle | les mots croisés (mpl) |
| editor | l'éditeur/l'éditrice; le rédacteur/la rédactrice |
| editorial | l'éditorial (m) |
| front page | la première page/à la une |
| *This article is on the front page!* | *Cet article est à la une!* |
| headline | le titre |
| newspaper | le journal |
| photo report | le photoreportage |
| press | la presse |
| press conference | la conférence de presse |
| publish | publier |
| read | lire |

| | |
|---|---|
| reader | **le lecteur/la lectrice** |
| report | **le reportage** |
| winner | **le lauréat/la lauréate** |
| *The winner of the prize was announced.* | *Le lauréat du prix a été annoncé.* |

## Newspaper Sections

## Les rubriques d'un journal

| | |
|---|---|
| Announcements | **Annonces** |
| Business section | **Finances/Entreprises** |
| Classified ads | **Petites Annonces** |
| Editorials | **Débats et Opinions** |
| Education | **Éducation** |
| Employment | **Emplois** |
| Entertainment | **Culture et Spectacles** |
| Fashion | **Mode** |
| Food and Drink | **Gastronomie** |
| Horoscope | **Horoscope** |
| International News | **Nouvelles Internationales** |
| Leisure | **Loisirs** |
| Lifestyle | **Art de Vivre** |
| *I find decorating ideas in the Lifestyle section.* | *Je trouve des idées de décoration dans la rubrique Art de Vivre.* |
| Local News | **Actualités** |
| Lottery, Lotto | **Loterie** |
| Movies | **Cinéma** |
| Obituaries | **Nécrologie** |
| Personal | **Courrier du Cœur** |
| Politics | **Politique** |
| Real Estate | **Immobilier** |
| Science and Health | **Sciences et Santé** |
| Sports | **Sports** |
| Stock Market | **Bourse** |
| Travel | **Voyages** |
| *The Travel section makes me dream.* | *La section des Voyages me fait rêver.* |

TV Guide                          Programme de télévision
Weather                          Météo(rologie)

# Fitness, Sports, and Outdoor Activities

## Exercise and Sports

## L'exercice et les sports

**INDIVIDUAL SPORTS**

**LES SPORTS INDIVIDUELS**

| | |
|---|---|
| aerobics | **l'aérobic (f)** |
| fitness training | **la musculation** |
| gymnastics | **la gymnastique** |
| jogging | **le jogging** |
| Rollerblade | **le patin à roulettes alignées/roller** |
| roller skate | **le patin à roulettes** |
| running | **le footing/le jogging** |
| skateboard | **le skateboard** |
| walking | **la marche** |
| *I go walking every morning before work.* | ***Je fais de la marche chaque matin avant le travail.*** |

**TEAM SPORTS**

**LES SPORTS D'ÉQUIPE**

| | |
|---|---|
| American football | **le football américain** |
| basketball | **le basket-ball/le basket** |
| handball | **le handball** |
| hockey | **le hockey** |
| rugby | **le rugby** |
| soccer | **le football/le foot** |
| volleyball | **le volley-ball/le volley** |

**AERIAL SPORTS**

**LES SPORTS DE L'AIR**

| | |
|---|---|
| bungee jumping | **le saut à l'élastique** |
| *Bungee jumping is for brave people.* | ***Le saut à l'élastique est pour les courageux.*** |
| extreme sport | **le sport extrême** |
| glide | **planer** |

| | |
|---|---|
| glider | le parapente/le deltaplane |
| hot-air balloon | la montgolfière |
| skydiving | le vol libre |

**AUTOMOBILE SPORTS**     **LES SPORTS AUTOMOBILES**

| | |
|---|---|
| automobile racing | l'autocross (m) |
| distance/road | le parcours |
| endurance | l'endurance (f) |
| karting | le karting |
| navigator | le navigateur |
| *The driver and the navigator make up a team.* | *Le pilote et le navigateur forment une équipe.* |
| racecar driver | le pilote |
| rally/race | le rallye |
| round/lap | le circuit |
| track | la piste |

**LAND SPORTS**     **LES SPORTS DE TERRE**

| | |
|---|---|
| all-terrain bike | le VTT (vélo tout terrain) |
| bike touring | le cyclotourisme |
| biking | le cyclisme |
| bowling (indoor) | le bowling |
| bowling (outdoor) | la pétanque |
| golf | le golf |
| horseback riding | l'équitation (f) |
| *They own a riding school.* | *Ils sont propriétaires d'une école d'équitation.* |
| judo | le judo |
| karate | le karaté |
| mountain climbing | l'escalade (f)/l'alpinisme (m) |
| outing on foot | la randonnée à pied |
| outing on horseback | la randonnée à cheval |
| outing on a bike | la randonnée en vélo |
| tennis | le tennis |
| *I go to many tennis tournaments.* | *Je vais à beaucoup de tournois de tennis.* |

## WINTER SPORTS

| | |
|---|---|
| alpine skiing | le ski alpin |
| cross-country skiing | le ski de fond |
| downhill race | la descente |
| figure skating | le patinage artistique |
| ice hockey | le hockey sur glace |
| ice skate | le patin à glace |
| ice-skating rink | la patinoire |
| luge | la luge |
| skate | patiner |
| ski | skier |
| *They go skiing in the Alps.* | *Ils vont skier dans les Alpes.* |
| ski jumping | le saut à ski |
| speed skating | le patinage de vitesse |

## LES SPORTS D'HIVER

## WATER SPORTS

| | |
|---|---|
| breast stroke | la brasse |
| butterfly stroke | le papillon |
| canoe | le canoë |
| crawl | le crawl |
| diving | la plongée |
| fishing | la pêche |
| Jet Ski | le Jet Ski |
| kayak | le kayak |
| kitesurfing | le kytesurf |
| pleasure boating | le yachting |
| *Pleasure boating is for sun lovers.* | *Le yachting est pour les accros du soleil.* |
| rowing | l'aviron (m) |
| sailing | la voile |
| surfing | le surf |
| swimming | la natation |
| underwater diving | la plongée sous-marine |
| wakeboarding | le wakeboard |
| water polo | le water-polo |

## LES SPORTS NAUTIQUES

| waterski | le ski nautique |
|---|---|
| windsurfing | la planche à voile |
| *There is windsurfing all along the Riviera.* | *On fait de la planche à voile tout le long de la Côte d'Azur.* |

## Competitions

## Les compétitions

| achievement | l'exploit (m) |
|---|---|
| athlete | l'athlète (m/f) |
| athletic | sportif/sportive |
| champion | le champion/la championne |
| championship | le championnat |
| club | le club |
| competitive | compétitif/compétitive |
| cup | la coupe |
| finish line | la ligne d'arrivée |
| fit | en forme |
| *She trains every day to stay fit.* | *Elle s'entraîne tous les jours pour rester en forme.* |
| lose | perdre |
| marathon | le marathon |
| race | la course |
| record | le record |
| sport | le sport |
| sports event | la manifestation sportive |
| tournament | le tournoi |
| train | s'entraîner |
| win | gagner |
| winner | le vainqueur; le/la gagnant(e) |

## Camping

## Le camping

| backpack | le sac à dos |
|---|---|
| barbecue | le barbecue |
| barbecue | rôtir/griller |

| battery | la pile |
| *Bring the battery-operated radio!* | *Apporte la radio à piles!* |
| cabin | le bungalow/le gîte |
| campfire | le feu de camp |
| camp | faire du camping |
| camper | le campeur/la campeuse |
| camping bed | le lit de camp |
| campground | le terrain de camping |
| camper (vehicle) | le camping-car/la caravane |
| candle | la bougie |
| disposable razor | le rasoir jetable |
| fire | le feu |
| *Let's make a campfire!* | *Faisons un feu de camp!* |
| first-aid kit | le kit de secours |
| hammock | le hamac |
| hot plate | le réchaud |
| inflatable pillow | l'oreiller gonflable (m) |
| lamp | la lampe |
| match | l'allumette (f) |
| mobile home | le mobil-home |
| mosquito repellent | le répulsif anti-moustique |
| mosquito net | la moustiquaire |
| outdoor | plein air |
| *In vacation camps, children enjoy outdoor activities.* | *Dans les colonies, les enfants jouissent d'activités en plein air.* |
| *sleep outdoors* | *dormir à la belle étoile* |
| sleeping bag | le sac de couchage |
| sunscreen | la crème solaire |
| Swiss army knife | le couteau suisse |
| tent | la tente |
| toiletry kit | la trousse de toilette |
| walking shoes | les chaussures de marche |
| water bottle | la gourde |

# Holidays

## Civil Holidays

April 1
April Fools' Day
book festival
Carnival
closing ceremonies
costume/disguise
dress up
dress up
*She makes herself beautiful for her date.*
Father's Day
firecrackers
fireworks
Labor Day
Mardi Gras
masquerade ball
Mother's Day
movie festival
music festival
*Every town has a music festival.*
National Holiday
New Year's Day
New Year's gifts
opening ceremonies
Valentine's Day

## Les fêtes civiles

le Jour du Poisson
poisson d'avril
la Fête du Livre
le Carnaval
la cérémonie de clôture
le costume/déguisement
se mettre sur son trente et un
se faire beau/belle
*Elle se fait belle pour son rendez-vous.*
la Fête des Pères
les pétards
les feux d'artifice
la Fête du Travail (le 1er mai)
le Mardi Gras
le bal masqué
la Fête des Mères
la Fête du Cinéma
la Fête de la Musique
*Chaque ville a une fête de la musique.*
la Fête Nationale (le 14 juillet)
le Nouvel An/la Saint-Sylvestre
les étrennes (fpl)
la cérémonie d'ouverture
la Saint-Valentin

## Religious Holidays

Christmas Eve
Christmas .
Christmas/New Year's Eve meal
Easter

## Les fêtes religieuses

la veille de Noël
Noël
le réveillon
Pâques

| | |
|---|---|
| *For Easter, shops sell chocolate chickens.* | *À Pâques les magasins vendent des poules en chocolat.* |
| Hanukkah | **Hanoukka** |
| menora | **la ménora** |
| Midnight Mass | **la messe de minuit** |
| Passover | **la Pâque juive** |
| Ramadan | **le Ramadan** |
| Sabbath | **le Sabbat** |
| Santa Claus | **le Père Noël/Papa Noël** |
| Yule log | **la bûche de Noël** |

# Other Pastimes

| **Eating Out** | **Les sorties au restaurant** |
|---|---|
| aperitif | **l'apéritif** |
| appetizer | **le hors-d'œuvre** |

 **Must-Know Tip**

Be careful not to mistake **l'apéritif** for a food appetizer. It is an alcoholic drink served before the meal. The French word for *appetizer* is **hors-d'œuvre**.

| | |
|---|---|
| bar | **le bar** |
| bill, check | **l'addition (f)** |
| Bon appétit! | **Bon appétit!** |
| cafeteria | **la cafétéria** |
| connoisseur | **le connaisseur** |
| *I am a wine connoisseur.* | *Je suis un connaisseur de vins.* |
| cooking | **la cuisine** |
| dessert | **le dessert** |
| dish | **le plat** |
| drink | **boire** |

| eat out | **sortir manger** |
|---------|-------------------|
| entrée | **l'entrée (f)** |

 **Must-Know Tip**

Be aware that in French, the word **entrée** is used to describe the dish served after a soup or appetizer, but before the main dish (usually meat). What Americans call an *entrée* is in fact **le plat principal** in French.

| feast on | **se régaler** |
|----------|----------------|
| food (art) | **la gastronomie** |
| menu | **la carte** |
| *The menu is on the table.* | *La carte est sur la table.* |

 **Must-Know Tip**

Be aware of the false cognate *menu*. While **la carte** is the *menu*, **le menu** is a meal featuring a small selection of options for appetizers, entrées, dessert, and often wine at a predetermined price.

| order | **commander** |
|-------|---------------|
| price | **le prix** |
| reservation | **la réservation** |
| restaurant | **le restaurant** |
| science of wine | **l'œnologie (f)** |
| self-service | **le self-service** |
| serve | **servir** |
| server | **le serveur/la serveuse** |
| special | **le menu du jour** |
| specialty | **la spécialité** |
| taste | **goûter** |
| *Taste this pâté!* | *Goûte ce pâté!* |
| tasting | **la dégustation** |

| tax | la taxe |
| tip | le pourboire |
| waiter | le garçon |
| waitress | la serveuse |

## Circuses and Fairs

## Le cirque et la foire

| acrobat | l'acrobate (m/f) |
| amusement park | la fête foraine |
| bumper cars | les autos tamponneuses (fpl) |
| carousel | le carrousel |
| circus | le cirque |
| clown | le clown |
| *The clown has a sad face.* | *Le clown a l'air triste.* |
| cotton candy | la barbe à papa |
| dove | la colombe |
| elephant | l'éléphant (m) |
| fair | la foire |
| horse | le cheval |
| hypnosis | l'hypnose (f) |
| hypnotize | hypnotiser |
| juggler | le jongleur |
| illusion | l'illusion (f) |
| illusionist | le prestidigitateur |
| levitate | léviter |
| *The illusionist's assistant levitates.* | *Le prestidigitateur fait léviter son assistante.* |
| | |
| magic | la magie |
| magic trick | le tour de magie |
| magician | le magicien/la magicienne |
| ride | le manège |
| roasted chestnuts | les marrons chauds (mpl) |
| tamer/trainer | le dompteur |
| tent | la tente |
| tightrope | la corde raide |

| | |
|---|---|
| trapeze artist | le/la trapéziste |
| *The trapeze artist swings gracefully.* | *La trapéziste se balance gracieusement.* |

## Hobbies and Games

## Les hobbies et les jeux

| | |
|---|---|
| bet | **le pari** |
| bet | **parier** |
| board games | **les jeux de société (mpl)** |
| camera (digital) | **l'appareil photo (m) (numérique)** |
| cards | **les cartes (fpl)** |
| checkers | **le jeu de dames** |
| chess | **les échecs (mpl)** |
| collect | **collectionner** |
| collection | **la collection** |
| crochet | **faire du crochet** |
| crossword puzzle | **les mots croisés (mpl)** |
| disco | **la discothèque** |
| distraction/entertainment | **le divertissement** |
| *You must balance work and distractions.* | *Il faut balancer le travail et les divertissements.* |
| exert oneself | **se dépenser** |
| exhibit | **l'exposition (f)** |
| film club | **le ciné-club** |
| fixing things/D.I.Y. projects | **le bricolage** |
| gambler | **le parieur** |
| game | **le jeu** |
| gardening | **le jardinage** |
| have fun | **s'amuser** |
| *Have fun, sweetheart!* | *Amuse-toi bien, chéri!* |
| horse race | **la course hippique** |
| knit | **tricoter/faire du tricot** |
| lottery | **la loterie** |
| leisure time | **le loisir** |
| nightclub | **la boîte de nuit** |

| | |
|---|---|
| passionate/crazy | **passionné(e)/fana/mordu(e)** |
| photography | **la photographie** |
| play | **jouer** |
| *What do you like to play?* | ***À quoi aimes-tu jouer?*** |
| recreation | **la distraction/la récréation** |
| relax | **se relaxer/se détendre** |

# 9

# *Getting Around*

# Transportation and Traffic

## Transportation

| English | Le transport |
|---|---|
| automobile | l'auto(mobile) (f) |
| bicycle | la bicyclette |
| bike | le vélo |
| board/get on | monter |
| boat | le bateau |
| bus | l'autobus (m)/le bus |
| bus (long distance) | l'autocar (m)/le car |
| bus depot | le garage d'autobus |
| bus ride | le trajet en autobus |
| *The bus ride only takes twenty minutes.* | *Le trajet en autobus ne dure que vingt minutes.* |
| bus stop | l'arrêt d'autobus (m) |
| car | la voiture |
| car ride | la promenade en voiture |
| get off | descendre |
| helmet | le casque |
| *means of transportation* | *les moyens de transport (mpl)* |
| motorcycle | la motocyclette/la moto |
| plane | l'avion (m) |
| *public transportation* | *les transports en commun (mpl)* |
| space shuttle | la navette spatiale |
| subway | le métro |
| subway station | la station de métro |
| stop | s'arrêter |
| train | le train |
| truck | le camion |
| van | le fourgon/la camionnette |
| vehicle | le véhicule |

## Cars

| | |
|---|---|
| air conditioner | **la climatisation** |
| automatic drive | **la boîte de changement de vitesse automatique** |
| automobile | **l'automobile/l'auto (f)** |
| battery | **la batterie** |
| blinker | **le clignotant** |
| *Use your blinkers!* | ***Sers-toi de tes clignotants!*** |
| brake | **le frein** |
| brake fluid | **le liquide pour freins** |
| breakdown | **la panne** |
| breakdown repair | **le dépannage** |
| bumper | **le pare-chocs** |
| car | **la voiture** |
| chassis | **la carrosserie** |
| clutch | **l'embrayage (m)** |
| dashboard | **le tableau de bord** |
| disengage clutch | **débrayer** |
| *I am practicing how to engage and disengage the clutch.* | ***Je m'entraîne à embrayer et débrayer.*** |
| door | **la portière** |
| engage clutch | **embrayer** |
| engine | **le moteur** |
| exhaust (pipe) | **le tuyau d'échappement** |
| fill up | **faire le plein** |
| forward/backward gear | **la marche avant/arrière** |
| gas | **l'essence (f)** |
| gas (diesel) | **le gazole/le gasoil** |
| gas (unleaded) | **sans-plomb** |
| gas pedal | **l'accélérateur (m)** |
| gas station | **la station-service** |
| gas tank | **le réservoir** |
| gear | **la vitesse** |

# Les voitures

| | |
|---|---|
| I am learning to shift gears without stalling. | J'apprends à changer de vitesse sans caler. |
| glove compartment | la boîte à gants |
| hand brake | le frein à main |
| headlight | le phare |
| hood | le capot |
| horn | le klaxon |
| Sound your horn! | Klaxonne! |
| ignition | l'allumage (m) |
| ignition key | la clef de contact |
| license plate | la plaque d'immatriculation |
| lights | l'éclairage (m) |
| lubricate | lubrifier |
| mechanic | le mécanicien/la mécanicienne |
| mileage | le kilométrage |
| mirror | le miroir |
| motor | le moteur |
| motor oil | l'huile (f) |
| An oil change is recommended. | Un changement d'huile est recommandé. |
| passenger | le passager/la passagère |
| pedal | la pédale |
| pump | la pompe |
| radiator | le radiateur |
| rear light | le feu arrière |
| rearview mirror | le rétroviseur |
| seat | le siège |
| seat belt | la ceinture de sécurité |
| Buckle your seat belt. | Attachez votre ceinture de sécurité. |
| spare tire | la roue de secours |
| spark plug | la bougie |
| speedometer | l'indicateur de vitesse (m)/le compteur |
| steering wheel | le volant |

| | |
|---|---|
| tire | le pneu |
| tow truck | la dépanneuse |
| transmission | la boîte de vitesse |
| trunk | le coffre |
| window | la vitre |
| windshield | le pare-brise |
| *The windshield is fogged up.* | *Le pare-brise est embué.* |
| windshield wiper | l'essuie-glace (m) |

## Traffic — La circulation

| | |
|---|---|
| accelerate | accélérer |
| accident | l'accident (m) |
| block | la rue/le quartier |
| circle (roundabout) | le rond-point |
| corner | le coin |
| cross | traverser |
| curve | le virage |
| cut off | faire une queue de poisson |
| detour | le détour/la déviation |
| direct traffic | diriger la circulation |
| drive | conduire |
| *Don't drive on icy roads.* | *Ne conduisez pas sur des routes verglacées.* |
| driver | le conducteur/la conductrice |
| driver (bus/taxi) | le chauffeur |
| driver's license | le permis de conduire |
| fine | l'amende (f) |
| highway | l'autoroute (f) |
| hill | la pente |
| lane | la voie |
| lane change | le changement de voie |
| map | la carte/le plan |
| one-way | sens unique (m) |
| park | stationner/se garer |

| | |
|---|---|
| parking | **le parking/le stationnement** |
| *No parking.* | ***Stationnement interdit.*** |
| parking meter | **le parcomètre** |
| pedestrian | **le piéton/la piétonne** |
| pedestrian crossing | **le passage à piétons** |
| road | **la route** |
| road signs | **la signalisation routière** |
| run over | **écraser** |
| sidewalk | **le trottoir** |
| signal | **signaler** |
| *I am signaling a turn.* | ***Je signale un changement de direction.*** |
| signals | **les feux de circulation (mpl)** |
| slow down | **ralentir** |
| speeding | **faire de l'excès de vitesse** |
| start | **démarrer** |
| stop | **s'arrêter** |
| straight ahead | **droit devant** |
| street | **la rue** |
| toll | **le péage** |
| traffic | **la circulation** |
| traffic jam | **le bouchon/l'embouteillage** |
| *We are late because of a traffic jam.* | ***Nous sommes en retard à cause d'un bouchon.*** |
| traffic light | **le feu** |
| traffic policeman | **l'agent de circulation (m)** |
| turn | **tourner** |
| turn left | **tourner à gauche** |
| turn right | **tourner à droite** |
| turnpike | **(auto)route à péage (f)** |
| U-turn | **le demi-tour** |
| warning | **l'avertissement (m)** |
| weave in | **zigzaguer/se frayer un chemin** |

# Tourism and Travel

## General Terms

all-inclusive

*This menu costs 20 euros all-inclusive.*

American plan

book (a flight, a room)

brochure


business trip

car rental agency

check-in

check-out


city map

city package

departure point

destination

*What is your destination?*

excursion

exotic

fare

get information

guide

guided tour

hitchhiking

information

inquire

package tour

*I prefer a package tour.*

plan

plan

pleasure trip

preparations

## Généralités

**tout compris**

***Ce menu coûte 20 euros tout compris.***

**pension complète**

**faire une réservation**

**le prospectus/le dépliant/la brochure**

**le voyage d'affaires**

**l'agence de location automobile (f)**

**l'enregistrement (m)**

**la vérification de sortie/le règlement des charges**

**le plan de la ville**

**le tour de ville**

**le point de départ**

**la destination**

***Quelle est votre destination?***

**l'excursion (f)**

**exotique**

**le tarif**

**s'informer**

**le/la guide**

**la visite guidée**

**faire de l'auto-stop**

**le renseignement**

**se renseigner**

**le voyage à forfait**

***Je préfère un voyage à forfait.***

**faire des projets**

**le projet**

**le voyage d'agrément**

**les préparatifs (mpl)**

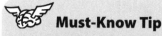
| | |
|---|---|
| promotion | **la promotion** |
| reservation | **la réservation** |
| schedule | **l'horaire (m)** |
| schedule | **programmer** |
| season | **la saison** |
| high season | **la pleine saison** |
| off-season | **hors-saison** |
| secluded | **isolé(e)** |
| site | **le site** |
| stay | **le séjour** |
| ticket | **le billet/le ticket** |
| nonrefundable ticket | **le billet non-remboursable** |
| one-way ticket | **l'aller simple (m)** |
| two-way ticket | **l'aller et retour (m)** |
| tourism | **le tourisme** |
| tourist | **le/la touriste** |
| tourist office | **le syndicat d'initiative/l'office du tourisme (m)** |
| touristic | **touristique** |
| travel | **voyager** |
| travel agency | **l'agence de voyage (f)** |
| travel agent | **l'agent de voyage (m)** |
| travel guide | **le guide touristique** |
| travel plan | **le projet de voyage** |
| traveler | **le voyageur/la voyageuse** |
| traveler's check | **le chèque de voyage** |
| vacation | **les vacances (fpl)** |
| *Our summer vacation starts in June.* | *Nos grandes vacances commencent en juin.* |

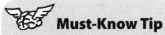
| | |
|---|---|
| vacationer | le vacancier/la vacancière |
| voucher | le bon d'échange |

## Travel Abroad — Les voyages à l'étranger

| | |
|---|---|
| abroad | à l'étranger |
| border | la frontière |
| currency exhange office | le bureau de change |
| currency | la devise |
| customs | la douane |
| declare | déclarer |
| *I do not have anything to declare.* | *Je n'ai rien à déclarer.* |
| duty | la taxe |
| duty-free | hors-taxe |
| exchange rate | le taux de change |
| expired | périmé(e) |
| immunization | la vaccination |
| immunization records | le carnet de santé |
| passport | le passeport |
| valid | valide |
| visa | le visa |

## Air Travel — Voyager en avion

### AT THE AIRPORT — À L'AÉROPORT

| | |
|---|---|
| air traffic control | le contrôle de l'air |
| airport | l'aéroport (m)/l'aérogare (f) |
| arrival | l'arrivée (f) |
| availability | la disponibilité |
| available | disponible |
| *Is there still a seat available?* | *Y a-t-il encore une place disponible?* |
| baggage tag | l'étiquette (f) |

| | |
|---|---|
| baggage claim | **la sortie des bagages** |
| behind schedule | **en retard** |
| boarding pass | **la carte d'embarquement** |
| business class | **la classe affaires/business/club** |
| cancellation | **l'annulation (f)** |
| check in | **enregistrer** |
| check-in desk | **le comptoir de l'enregistrement** |
| coach | **la classe économie** |
| complaint | **la réclamation** |
| control tower | **la tour de contrôle** |
| conveyor belt | **le tapis roulant** |
| courtesy shuttle | **la navette gratuite** |
| *The hotel provides a courtesy shuttle.* | *L'hôtel procure une navette gratuite.* |
| delay | **le retard** |
| direct flight | **le vol direct** |
| discounted fare | **le tarif soldé/dégriffé** |
| domestic flight | **le vol domestique** |
| frequent flyer | **le voyageur fréquent** |
| gate | **la porte d'embarquement** |
| international flight | **le vol international** |
| jet | **le jet/l'avion à réaction (m)** |
| land | **atterrir** |
| landing | **l'atterrissage (m)** |
| *There was an emergency landing at Roissy.* | *Il y a eu un atterrissage forcé à Roissy.* |
| landing strip | **la piste d'atterrissage** |
| load | **charger** |
| lost and found | **les objets trouvés (mpl)** |
| luggage | **les bagages (mpl)** |
| luggage hold | **la soute à bagages** |
| *hand luggage* | *les bagages à main* |
| meal service | **le service repas** |
| miss (a flight) | **rater/manquer (un vol)** |
| nonstop | **sans escale** |
| on schedule | **à l'heure** |
| overbooking | **la surréservation** |

| | |
|---|---|
| rerouting | **le changement d'itinéraire** |
| safety measures | **les mesures de sûreté (fpl)** |
| security | **la sécurité** |
| security check | **le contrôle de sécurité** |
| standby list | **la liste d'attente** |
| stop over | **faire escale** |
| *The plane makes a stopover in Montréal.* | ***L'avion fait escale à Montréal.*** |
| stopover | **l'escale (f)** |
| suitcase | **la valise** |
| take off | **décoller** |
| takeoff | **le décollage** |
| terminal | **le terminal** |
| ticket agent | **l'agent d'enregistrement (m)** |
| upgrade | **le surclassement** |

| **ON THE PLANE** | **DANS L'AVION** |
|---|---|
| aircraft | **l'avion (m)** |
| air-conditioning | **l'air conditionné (m)** |
| air pressure | **la pression de l'oxygène** |
| airsickness | **le mal de l'air** |
| *The drop in air pressure causes airsickness.* | ***La baisse de pression de l'oxygène cause le mal de l'air.*** |
| aisle | **l'allée centrale (f)** |
| altitude | **l'altitude (f)** |
| beverage service | **le service bar** |
| blanket | **la couverture** |
| *Boarding now!* | ***Embarquement immédiat!*** |
| cabin | **la cabine** |
| cockpit | **la cabine de pilotage** |
| copilot | **le copilote** |
| crew | **l'équipage (m)** |
| economy class | **la classe touriste/économie** |
| emergency | **l'urgence (f)** |
| *In case of emergency, put on the oxygen mask!* | ***En cas d'urgence, mettre le masque à oxygène!*** |

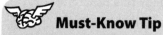
| | |
|---|---|
| emergency exit | **la sortie de secours** |
| exit | **la sortie** |
| extra-large baggage | **bagages hors format (m)** |
| fasten | **attacher** |
| first class | **la première classe** |
| flight attendant | **le steward/l'hôtesse de l'air** |
| flight time | **la durée du vol** |
| fly | **voler** |
| headset | **les écouteurs (mpl)** |
| jet lag (have) | **souffrir du décalage horaire** |
| *I always have jet lag.* | *Je souffre toujours dû au décalage horaire.* |
| | |
| lavatory | **les toilettes (fpl)** |
| life jacket | **le gilet de sauvetage** |
| main cabin | **la cabine principale** |
| nonsmoking | **non fumeur** |
| on board | **à bord** |
| overhead compartment | **le coffre à bagages** |
| pillow | **l'oreiller (m)** |
| pilot | **le pilote** |
| rear of the plane | **l'arrière de l'avion (m)** |
| row | **la rangée** |
| seat | **la place** |
| *I prefer an aisle seat.* | *Je préfère une place dans l'allée centrale.* |
| | |
| seatbelt | **la ceinture de sécurité** |
| time lag | **le décalage horaire** |
| turbulence | **la turbulence** |
| vegetarian meal | **le plat végétarien** |
| window | **la fenêtre/le hublot** |

## Travel by Train

| | |
|---|---|
| aisle | **le couloir** |
| baggage checkroom | **la consigne** |
| berth | **la couchette** |
| cabin | **le compartiment** |
| Channel tunnel | **Eurotunnel** |
| commuter pass | **l'abonnement (m)** |
| *A commuter pass is the best solution.* | *Un abonnement est la meilleure formule.* |
| conductor | **le contrôleur** |
| connection | **la correspondance** |
| delay update | **le bulletin de retard** |
| express train | **le train direct/le rapide** |
| first class | **première classe** |
| high-speed train | **le train à grande vitesse (TGV)** |
| locomotive | **la locomotive** |
| night train | **le train de nuit** |
| platform | **le quai** |
| *Our train leaves from this platform.* | *Notre train part de ce quai.* |
| restaurant | **le wagon-restaurant** |
| rail | **le rail** |
| *by rail* | *par le train/en train* |
| railroad crossing | **le passage à niveau** |
| railroad track | **la voie ferrée** |
| railway line | **la ligne des chemins de fer** |
| reduced-fare pass | **la carte de réduction** |
| seat | **la place** |
| service | **desservir** |
| *This train station services the northeast only.* | *Cette gare dessert seulement le nord-est.* |
| sleeping car | **le wagon-lit** |
| tourist class | **deuxième classe** |
| train | **le train** |
| train station | **la gare** |
| train station restaurant | **le buffet de la gare** |

## Voyager en train

| | |
|---|---|
| tunnel | **le tunnel** |
| validate | **composter** |

## Travel by Boat

## Voyager en bateau

| | |
|---|---|
| berthed | **amarré(e)** |
| boat | **le bateau** |
| bow | **la proue** |
| bridge | **la passerelle** |
| cabin | **la cabine** |
| *I want a cabin on the upper deck.* | ***Je veux une cabine sur le pont supérieur.*** |
| | |
| porthole | **le hublot** |
| captain | **le capitaine** |
| choppy | **agité(e)** |
| cruise | **la croisière** |
| deck | **le pont** |
| deckchair | **le transatlantique** |
| dock | **arrimer** |
| ferryboat | **le bac** |
| float | **flotter** |
| *A life jacket helps you float.* | ***Un gilet de sauvetage vous aide à flotter.*** |
| | |
| harbor | **la gare maritime** |
| island | **l'île (f)** |
| lifebelt | **la ceinture de sauvetage** |
| lifeboat | **le canot de sauvetage** |
| life-buoy | **la bouée de sauvetage** |
| life vest | **le gilet de sauvetage** |
| ocean liner | **le paquebot** |
| overboard | **par-dessus bord** |
| *man overboard* | ***un homme à la mer*** |
| pier | **le quai** |
| port | **le port** |
| river cruise | **la croisière fluviale** |

| | |
|---|---|
| sailboat | **le bateau à voiles** |
| sea | **la mer** |
| seaman | **le matelot** |
| seaport | **le port marin** |
| seasickness | **le mal de mer** |
| *I am seasick.* | *J'ai le mal de mer.* |
| ship (cargo) | **la péniche** |
| ship (military) | **le navire** |
| stern | **la poupe** |
| tide | **la marée** |
| yacht | **le yacht** |

# Accommodations and Hotels

| **Accommodations** | **Formules de logement** |
|---|---|
| accommodate | **loger** |
| amenities | **les services** |
| boarding house | **la pension** |
| book | **réserver** |
| charge | **les frais (mpl)** |
| cottage | **le chalet** |
| *We are renting a cottage in the Alps.* | *Nous louons un chalet dans les Alpes.* |
| country lodging | **le gîte** |
| efficiency | **logement avec cuisine** |
| fire exit | **la sortie de secours** |
| guest | **le/la client(e)** |
| guest room | **la chambre d'hôte** |
| inn | **l'auberge (f)** |
| motel | **le motel** |
| resort (spa) | **la station thermale** |
| resort (seaside) | **la station balnéaire** |
| resort (winter sports) | **la station des sports d'hiver** |
| star | **l'étoile (f)** |

| | |
|---|---|
| tent | la tente |
| vacation camp | la colonie de vacances |
| *This summer I will be a camp counselor.* | *Cet été je serai moniteur dans une colonie de vacances.* |
| vacation club | le club de vacances |
| youth hostel | l'auberge de jeunesse (f) |

## Hotels

## Les hôtels

| | |
|---|---|
| beauty salon | le salon de beauté |
| bellboy | le groom |
| bill | la note |
| breakfast room | la salle des petits déjeuners |
| check in | s'enregistrer |
| check out | payer/régler la facture |
| elevator | l'ascenseur (m) |
| freight elevator | l'ascenseur de service (m) |
| front desk | la réception |
| *Where is the front desk manager?* | *Où est le chef de réception?* |
| hotel owner | l'hôtelier/l'hôtelière |
| laundromat | la laverie automatique |
| laundry service | le service de blanchisserie |
| lobby | le hall |
| lounge | le salon |
| luxury hotel | un hôtel de luxe |
| *a three-star hotel* | *un hôtel à trois étoiles* |
| night | la nuit |
| pool | la piscine |
| rate | le prix/le tarif |
| *Breakfast is included in the daily rate.* | *Le petit déjeuner est compris dans le tarif.* |
| reception | la réception |
| *room and board* | *la pension complète* |
| room service | le service étage/le service de chambre |

| spa | le sauna |
| staff | le personnel |
| suite | la suite |
| tip | le pourboire |
| vacant | disponible/libre |
| valet parking attendant | le voiturier |

## Rooms / Les chambres

| balcony | le balcon |
| bathroom | la salle de bains |
| comfortable | confortable |
| connectivity charge | les frais de téléphone |
| disturb | déranger |
| *Do not disturb!* | *Ne pas déranger!* |
| double bed | le grand lit |
| room (double) | la chambre à deux lits |
| room (single) | la chambre simple |
| safe | le coffre-fort |
| soundproof | insonorisé(e) |
| suite | la suite |
| terrace | la terrasse |
| twin beds | des lits jumeaux |
| view | la vue |
| *I want a room with a view of the sea.* | *Je veux une chambre avec vue sur la mer.* |
| wireless Internet | Internet sans fil |

# 10

# *Society and Government*

# Rights and Legal Status

| | |
|---|---|
| birth certificate | **l'extrait de naissance** |
| citizen | **le/la citoyen(ne)** |
| citizenship | **le civisme** |
| *He shows good citizenship.* | *Il fait preuve de civisme.* |
| cultural identity | **l'identité culturelle** |
| deportation | **la déportation** |
| deported | **déporté(e)** |
| discrimination | **la discrimination** |
| dual nationality | **la double nationalité** |
| exclusion | **l'exclusion (f)** |
| expatriation | **l'expatriation (f)** |
| expatriated | **expatrié(e)** |
| *Expatriated French citizens still have the right to vote.* | *Les Français expatriés ont toujours le droit de vote.* |
| expulsion | **l'expulsion (f)** |
| foreigner | **l'étranger/l'étrangère** |
| French (by origin) | **le Français/la Française de souche** |
| identification card | **la carte d'identité** |
| illegal immigrant | **le/la clandestin(e)** |
| immigrant | **l'immigrant(e)** |
| immigration | **l'immigration (f)** |
| integrate | **s'intégrer** |
| intolerance | **l'intolérance (f)** |
| minority | **la minorité** |
| nationality | **la nationalité** |
| naturalization | **la naturalisation** |
| *I am now eligible for naturalization.* | *J'ai maintenant droit à la naturalisation.* |
| origin | **l'origine (f)** |
| passport | **le passeport** |
| political asylum | **l'asile politique (m)** |

| | |
|---|---|
| prejudice | **le préjugé** |
| preserve one's customs | **préserver ses coutumes** |
| racism | **le racisme** |
| refugee | **le/la réfugié(e)** |
| residence permit | **le permis de séjour** |
| *Illegal immigrants dream of obtaining a residence permit.* | ***Les immigrants clandestins rêvent d'obtenir un permis de séjour.*** |
| right of asylum | **le droit d'asile** |
| *right to citizenship through lineage* | ***le droit du sang*** |
| *right to citizenship through place of birth* | ***le droit du sol*** |
| society | **la société** |
| tolerance | **la tolérance** |
| undocumented | **sans papiers** |
| work permit | **le permis de travail** |

# Law and Order

## System of Justice     Le système judiciaire

| | |
|---|---|
| acquit | **acquitter** |
| appeal | **faire appel** |
| *The death row convict is making an appeal.* | ***Le condamné à mort fait appel.*** |
| break the law | **violer la loi** |
| charge | **inculper** |
| condamn | **condamner** |
| convict | **le/la condamné(e)** |
| court of first instance | **la cour de première instance** |
| court of law | **la cour de justice** |
| criminal court | **le tribunal correctionnel** |
| *appear before a court* | ***comparaître en justice*** |
| custody pending trial | **la détention provisoire** |
| death penalty | **la peine de mort** |

| | |
|---|---|
| *The death penalty does not exist in France or in Canada.* | *La peine de mort n'existe ni en France ni au Canada.* |
| defense lawyer/counsel | **l'avocat de la défense (m)** |
| dismissal of charges | **le non-lieu** |
| DNA test | **le test ADN** |
| evidence/deposition | **la déposition** |
| fingerprints | **les empreintes digitales (fpl)** |
| *for the defense* | *à décharge* |
| *for the prosecution* | *à charge* |
| freedom | **la liberté** |
| guilt | **la culpabilité** |
| *The guilt of the accused must be proven.* | *Il faut prouver la culpabilité de l'inculpé.* |
| guilty | **coupable** |
| *not guilty* | *non coupable* |
| imprisonment | **l'emprisonnement (m)** |
| *life imprisonment* | *la réclusion à perpétuité* |
| illegal | **illégal(e)** |
| innocence | **l'innocence (f)** |
| innocent | **innocent(e)** |
| judge | **le juge d'instruction** |
| juror | **le/la juré(e)** |
| jury | **le jury** |
| law student | **l'étudiant(e) en droit** |
| law | **la loi** |

 **Must-Know Tip**

Be aware that though the term **loi** means *law*, the term **droit** is used to refer to the *field of law*.

| | |
|---|---|
| legal | **légal(e)** |
| *This is a legal document.* | *C'est un document légal.* |
| oath | **le serment** |

| plead | **plaider** |
| prison sentence | **la peine de prison** |
| prisoner | **le prisonnier/la prisonnière** |
| prosecutor | **le procureur** |
| respect | **respecter** |
| self-defense | **la légitime défense** |
| *In a case of self-defense, laws are more lenient.* | *Dans un cas de légitime défense, les lois sont plus indulgentes.* |
| sentence | **la sentence** |
| Supreme Court | **la Cour de Cassation** |
| suspended | **avec sursis** |
| testimony | **le témoignage** |
| trial | **le procès** |
| tribunal | **le tribunal** |
| verdict | **le jugement** |
| witness | **le témoin** |
| *They are calling the witnesses for the defense.* | *Ils appellent les témoins à décharge.* |

## Law Enforcement / Les forces de l'ordre

| apprehend | **appréhender** |
| armed police officer | **le gendarme** |
| arrest | **arrêter** |
| commissioner | **le commissaire** |
| cop | **le flic** |
| detective | **le détective** |
| imprison | **emprisonner** |
| incarcerate | **incarcérer** |
| inspector | **l'inspecteur/l'inspectrice** |
| investigate | **mener l'enquête** |
| investigation | **l'enquête (f)** |
| *The investigation is in progress.* | *L'enquête est en cours.* |
| police station | **le commissariat/le poste de police** |
| police | **la police** |
| policeman/woman | **l'agent de police (m)** |

## Crime

| | |
|---|---|
| accomplice | **le/la complice** |
| arson | **l'incendie volontaire (m)** |
| arsonist | **l'incendiaire (m/f)** |
| blackmail | **faire chanter** |
| blackmail | **le chantage** |
| blackmailer | **le maître-chanteur** |
| burglar | **le cambrioleur/la cambrioleuse** |
| burglarize | **cambrioler** |
| burglary | **le cambriolage** |
| *The police are investigating a series of burglaries.* | ***La police mène une enquête concernant une série de cambriolages.*** |
| *charged with a crime* | ***inculpé(e)*** |
| criminal | **le/la criminel(le)** |
| criminal record | **le casier judiciaire** |
| custody | **la garde à vue** |
| drug traffic | **le trafic des drogues** |
| embezzlement | **le détournement de fonds** |
| falsify | **falsifier** |
| felon | **le/la délinquant(e)** |
| felony | **l'acte de délinquance (m)** |
| forgery | **la contrefaçon** |
| gangster | **le gangster** |
| harassment | **le harcèlement** |
| *Sexual harassment is against the law.* | ***Le harcèlement sexuel est contre la loi.*** |
| homicide | **l'assassinat (m)** |
| juvenile crime | **la délinquance juvénile** |
| kidnap | **kidnapper/enlever** |
| kidnapping | **l'enlèvement (m)** |
| kill | **tuer/assassiner** |
| manslaughter | **l'homicide involontaire (m)** |
| misdemeanor | **le délit** |
| *He was caught in the act.* | ***Il a été pris en flagrant délit.*** |

## Le crime

| | |
|---|---|
| *murder in the first degree* | *l'assassinat* (m) |
| *murder in the second degree* | *le meurtre* |
| murderer | l'assassin (m) |
| murderer | le meurtrier/la meurtrière |
| pedophile | le/la pédophile |
| prowl | rôder |
| prowler | le rôdeur/la rôdeuse |
| rape | le viol |
| rape | violer |
| rapist | le violeur |
| repeat offender | le/la récidiviste |
| *Repeat offenders get heavier sentences.* | *Les récidivistes reçoivent des peines plus dures.* |
| shoplifting | le vol à l'étalage |
| steal | voler |
| swindler | l'escroc (m) |
| thief | le voleur/la voleuse |
| vandal | le/la vandale |
| vandalism | le vandalisme |
| white-collar crime | l'infraction administrative (f) |

# Government and Politics

| **Principles and Distribution of Power** | **Principes et distribution des pouvoirs** |
|---|---|
| Bill of Rights | la Déclaration des Droits de l'Homme |
| bill | le projet de loi |
| capitalism | le capitalisme |
| chauvinism | le chauvinisme |
| citizen | le citoyen/la citoyenne |
| confederation | la confédération |

| | |
|---|---|
| constitution | **la constitution** |
| democracy | **la démocratie** |
| democratic | **démocratique** |
| *We have a democratic government.* | *Nous avons un gouvernement démocratique.* |
| equality | **l'égalité (f)** |
| executive power | **le pouvoir exécutif** |
| fatherland | **la patrie** |
| federalism | **le fédéralisme** |
| fraternity | **la fraternité** |
| government | **le gouvernement** |
| judicial power | **le pouvoir judiciaire** |
| law | **la loi** |
| legislative power | **le pouvoir législatif** |
| liberty | **la liberté** |
| *"Liberty, Equality, Fraternity" is the French motto.* | *«Liberté, Egalité, Fraternité» est la devise de la France.* |
| nation | **la nation** |
| national | **national** |
| National Assembly | **l'Assemblée Nationale** |

 **Must-Know Tip**

Remember that most nouns and adjectives ending in **-al** form their plural by using **-aux,** as in **national/nationaux.**

| | |
|---|---|
| nationalism | **le nationalisme** |
| patriotism | **le patriotisme** |
| republic | **la république** |
| state | **l'état** |

## Elections | ## Les élections

| | |
|---|---|
| abstain | **s'abstenir** |
| ballot (sheet) | **le bulletin de vote** |
| ballot/voting | **le scrutin** |

| | |
|---|---|
| blank ballot | **le bulletin blanc** |
| candidate | **le/la candidat(e)** |
| *The candidate from the left won.* | *Le candidat de la gauche a gagné.* |
| count the ballots | **dépouiller le scrutin** |
| elect | **élire** |
| elected | **élu(e)** |
| election district | **la circonscription** |
| in a runoff | **en ballotage** |
| invalid ballot | **le bulletin nul** |
| presidential | **présidentiel(le)** |
| round of voting | **un tour de scrutin** |
| *suffrage by absolute majority* | *suffrage majoritaire* |
| universal suffrage | **le suffrage universel** |
| *This president was elected by universal suffrage.* | *Ce président a été élu au suffrage universel.* |
| voice/vote/suffrage | **la voix** |
| vote | **voter** |
| voter | **l'électeur/l'électrice** |

## Political Parties and Ideologies

## Les partis et les idéologies politiques

| | |
|---|---|
| alliance | **l'alliance (f)** |
| coalition | **la coalition** |
| communist | **communiste** |
| conservative | **conservateur/conservatrice** |
| dictatorship | **la dictature** |
| in the majority | **majoritaire** |
| in the minority | **minoritaire** |
| independent | **indépendant(e)** |
| initiative | **l'initiative (f)** |

| | |
|---|---|
| *The socialist party started a new initiative.* | *Le parti socialiste a lancé une nouvelle initiative.* |
| left | la gauche |
| liberal | libéral(e) |
| measure | la mesure |
| opposition | l'opposition (f) |
| party | le parti |
| program | le programme |
| regime | le régime |
| repression | la répression |
| right | la droite |
| socialist | socialiste |
| totalitarian | totalitaire |

## Politicians and Leaders — Les politiciens et les leaders

| | |
|---|---|
| cabinet | le conseil des ministres |
| deputy | le député |
| dictator | le dictateur |
| head of government/state | le chef d'état |
| *Heads of government have heavy responsibilities.* | *Les chefs d'état ont de lourdes responsabilités.* |
| leader | le/la dirigeant(e); le leader |
| minister | le ministre |
| politician | l'homme/la femme politique; le/la politicien(ne) |
| president | le président/la présidente |
| prime minister | le premier ministre |
| secretary of state | le/la secrétaire d'Etat |
| term | le mandat |
| vice president | le vice-président/la vice-présidente |

## Civil Administration — L'administration civile

| | |
|---|---|
| bureaucracy | la bureaucratie |
| capital city | la capitale |

| | |
|---|---|
| city hall | l'hôtel de ville (m) |
| civil servant | le/la fonctionnaire |
| county/administrative division | le département |
| function/office/duty | la fonction |
| *He performs his duty with much integrity.* | *Il exerce sa fonction avec beaucoup d'intégrité.* |
| mayor | le maire |
| mother country (France) | la métropole |
| overseas department | D.O.M. (département d'outre-mer) |
| *Martinique is an overseas department.* | *La Martinique est un département d'outre-mer.* |
| overseas territories | T.O.M. (territoires d'outre-mer) |
| public administration | l'administration publique (f) |
| region | la région |
| sales tax | taxe sur la valeur ajoutée (TVA) (f) |
| subunit of a department | l'arrondissement (m) |
| subunit of an *arrondissement* | le canton |
| tax authorities | le fisc |
| *Tax authorities can impose heavy fines.* | *Le fisc peut imposer de lourdes amendes.* |
| tax collector | le percepteur/la perceptrice |
| tax declaration | la déclaration d'impôts |
| taxable | imposable |
| taxes | les impôts (mpl) |
| taxpayer | le/la contribuable |
| town hall | la mairie |
| township | la commune |

# On the International Scene

| **International Relations** | **Les relations internationales** |
|---|---|
| agreement | l'accord (m) |
| alliance | l'alliance (f) |

| | |
|---|---|
| ally | l'allié(e) |
| ambassador | l'ambassadeur/l'ambassadrice |
| bilateral meetings | les réunions bilatérales (fpl) |
| conference | la conférence |
| conflict | le conflit |
| confrontation | la confrontation |
| consul | le consul |
| consulate | le consulat |
| cooperate | coopérer |
| cooperation | la coopération |
| crisis | la crise |
| detente | la détente |
| diplomacy | la diplomatie |
| diplomat | le/la diplomate |
| diplomatic | diplomatique |
| *Diplomatic efforts will preserve peace.* | *Les efforts diplomatiques assureront la paix.* |
| disagreement | le désaccord |
| embargo | l'embargo (m) |
| embassy | l'ambassade (f) |
| *The American embassy is near the Louvre.* | *L'ambassade américaine est près du Louvre.* |
| foreign policy | la politique étrangère |
| intervention | l'intervention (f) |
| meeting | la réunion |
| *summit meeting* | *la réunion au sommet* |
| neutrality | la neutralité |
| *Switzerland proved its neutrality.* | *La Suisse a prouvé sa neutralité.* |
| pact | le pacte |
| partnership | le jumelage |
| power | la puissance |
| pressure | la pression |
| quarrel | la querelle |
| reconciliation, rapprochement | le rapprochement |

| | |
|---|---|
| reconciliation | **la réconciliation** |
| sanction | **la sanction** |
| *Sanctions were imposed to pressure the dictator.* | ***On a imposé des sanctions pour faire pression sur le dictateur.*** |
| talk | **l'entretien (m)** |
| tension | **la tension** |
| treaty | **le traité** |
| understanding | **l'entente (f)** |
| union | **l'union (f)** |

## War and Peace — ## La guerre et la paix

| | |
|---|---|
| aggression | **l'agression (f)** |
| armament/arms | **l'armement (m)** |
| attack | **attaquer** |
| attack | **l'attaque (f)** |
| capitulation | **la capitulation** |
| civil war | **la guerre civile** |
| *Hemingway reported on the civil war in Spain.* | ***Hemingway a fait des reportages sur la guerre civile en Espagne.*** |
| concentration camp | **le camp de concentration** |
| conscientious objector | **l'objecteur de conscience (m)** |
| dead (person) | **le/la mort(e)** |
| declaration | **la déclaration** |
| defeat | **la défaite** |
| defense | **la défense** |
| deserter | **le déserteur** |
| disarmament | **le désarmement** |
| enemy | **l'ennemi (m)** |
| evacuation | **l'évacuation (f)** |
| hostilities | **les hostilités (fpl)** |
| *Hostilities caused the evacuation of foreign tourists.* | ***Les hostilités ont causé l'évacuation des touristes étrangers.*** |
| invasion | **l'invasion (f)** |
| losses | **les pertes** |

| | |
|---|---|
| pacifism | le pacifisme |
| pacifist | le/la pacifiste |
| peace | la paix |
| proliferation | la prolifération |
| resistance | la résistance |
| *state of emergency* | *l'état d'urgence* (m) |
| surrender | se rendre |
| treason | la trahison |
| *Treason is a capital crime.* | *La trahison est un crime capital.* |
| ultimatum | l'ultimatum (m) |
| victory | la victoire |
| war crime | le crime de guerre |
| war criminal | le criminel de guerre |
| wounded | le/la blessé(e) |

## Military Power      La force de frappe militaire

| | |
|---|---|
| aircraft carrier | le porte-avions |
| airstrike | la frappe aérienne |
| armed forces | les forces armées |
| artillery | l'artillerie (f) |
| bomb | la bombe |
| bombardment | le bombardement |
| *Entire towns were destroyed during bombardments.* | *Des villes entières ont été détruites pendant les bombardements.* |
| bomblet | la minibombe |
| coalition forces | les forces de coalition (fpl) |
| cruise missile | le missile de croisière |
| destroy | détruire |
| explode | exploser |
| fighter plane | l'avion de chasse (m) |
| firepower | la puissance de feu |
| grenade launchers | les lance-grenades |
| mine | la mine |
| minesweeper | le dragueur de mines |

| | |
|---|---|
| missile | **la fusée/le missile** |
| *The ship is equipped with missiles.* | ***Le navire est équipé de missiles.*** |
| gun | **le pistolet/le revolver** |
| machine gun | **la mitraillette** |
| pound | **pilonner** |
| range | **le rayon d'action** |
| rifle | **le fusil** |
| sabotage | **le sabotage** |
| sharpshooter | **le tireur d'élite** |
| shell | **l'obus (m)** |
| spy satellite | **le satellite-espion** |
| strike force | **la force de frappe** |
| submarine | **le sous-marin** |
| *The navy is deploying its submarines.* | ***La marine déploie ses sous-marins.*** |
| tank | **le char** |

## Military Personnel and Organizations / Le personnel et l'organisation militaire

| | |
|---|---|
| air force | **l'armée de l'air (f)** |
| battalion | **le bataillon** |
| commander-in-chief | **le commandant en chef** |
| conscript | **le conscrit** |
| division | **la division** |
| general | **le général** |
| ground forces | **l'armée de terre (f)** |
| infantry | **l'infanterie (f)** |
| medical support | **le support médical** |
| militiaman | **le milicien** |
| military service | **le service militaire** |
| navy | **la marine (militaire)** |
| officer | **l'officier (m)** |
| professional army | **l'armée de métier** |
| recruit | **la recrue** |
| soldier | **le soldat** |

| | |
|---|---|
| troops | **les troupes** |
| volunteer | **le/la volontaire** |
| *France has an army made up of volunteers.* | ***La France a une armée composée de volontaires.*** |

## Terrorism
## Le terrorisme

| | |
|---|---|
| bomb | **la bombe** |
| *car bombing* | ***la voiture piégée*** |
| *detonate a bomb* | ***faire sauter une bombe*** |
| *letter bomb* | ***la lettre piégée*** |
| *time bomb* | ***la bombe à retardement*** |
| collapse | **l'effondrement (m)** |
| crash | **le crash** |
| explosive | **l'explosif (m)** |
| *remote-controlled explosive* | ***un explosif télécommandé*** |
| fear | **la peur** |
| gun down | **abattre** |
| gun | **le revolver/le pistolet** |
| hijacked plane | **l'avion détourné** |
| *The hijacked plane safely landed.* | ***L'avion détourné a atterri sain et sauf.*** |
| hijacking | **le détournement** |
| hoax | **le canular** |
| hostage | **l'otage (m)** |
| kidnapper | **le ravisseur/la ravisseuse** |
| lack of security | **l'insécurité (f)** |
| panic | **la panique** |
| rescue operation | **l'opération de sauvetage (f)** |
| search | **fouiller** |
| security | **la sécurité** |
| *Bags are searched to ensure the security of travelers.* | ***On fouille les valises pour assurer la sécurité des voyageurs.*** |
| sniper | **le tireur fou/la tireuse folle** |
| suicide attack | **l'attaque suicide (f)** |

| | |
|---|---|
| terrorist attack | **l'attentat terroriste (m)** |
| terrorist network | **le réseau terroriste** |
| terrorized | **terrorisé(e)** |
| track down | **traquer** |
| traumatic | **traumatisant(e)** |
| victim | **la victime** |

# 11

# *Nature and the Environment*

# Our Planet

## Space / L'espace

| Space | L'espace |
|---|---|
| air | l'air (m) |
| *There is a draft in this room.* | *Il y a un courant d'air dans cette chambre.* |
| astronaut | l'astronaute (m/f) |
| atmosphere | l'atmosphère (f) |
| attract | attirer |
| attraction | l'attraction (f) |
| celestial body | l'astre (m) |
| comet | la comète |
| constellation | la constellation |
| cosmonaut | le/la cosmonaute |
| eclipse | l'éclipse (f) |
| extraterrestrial | l'extraterrestre (m/f) |
| *I have never seen any extraterrestrials.* | *Je n'ai jamais vu d'extraterrestres.* |
| flying saucer | la soucoupe volante |
| galaxy | la galaxie |
| gravitate | graviter |
| light-year | l'année-lumière (f) |
| lunar | lunaire |
| meteor | le météore |
| Milky Way | la Voie lactée |
| moon | la lune |
| *The moon is a satellite of the earth.* | *La lune est un satellite de la terre.* |
| orbit | l'orbite (f) |
| oxygen | l'oxygène (m) |
| rocket | la fusée |
| rotation | la rotation |
| satellite | le satellite |
| sky | le ciel |
| solar system | le système solaire |
| spaceship | le vaisseau spatial |

| | |
|---|---|
| spatial | **spatial(e)** |
| star | **l'étoile (f)** |
| *Shooting stars bring good luck.* | *Les étoiles filantes portent bonheur.* |
| time zone | **le fuseau horaire** |
| UFO (unidentified flying object) | **l'OVNI (objet volant non identifié)** |
| universal | **universel(le)** |
| universe | **l'univers (m)** |
| weightlessness | **l'apesanteur (f)** |

## Earth

## La terre

**LAND**

**LA TERRE**

| | |
|---|---|
| altitude | **l'altitude (f)** |
| atlas | **l'atlas (m)** |
| basin | **le bassin** |
| border | **la frontière** |
| cave | **la grotte** |
| cliff | **la falaise** |
| coast | **la côte** |
| coastal area | **le littoral** |
| *This coastal area is made up of rocky beaches.* | *Ce littoral comporte des plages de galets.* |
| continent | **le continent** |
| country | **le pays** |
| countryside | **la campagne** |
| desert | **le désert** |
| desolate | **désertique** |
| dune | **la dune** |
| forest | **la forêt** |
| glacier | **le glacier** |
| gorge | **la gorge** |
| hill | **la colline** |
| island | **l'île (f)** |
| landscape | **le paysage** |

| | |
|---|---|
| *This landscape is very flat.* | *Ce paysage est très plat.* |
| maritime | **maritime** |
| mountain pass | **le col** |
| mountain | **la montagne** |
| nature | **la nature** |
| peak | **le sommet** |
| peninsula | **la péninsule** |
| plain | **la plaine** |
| plateau | **le plateau** |
| region | **la région** |
| relief | **le relief** |
| rock | **le rocher** |
| rocky | **rocheux/rocheuse** |
| *Corsica is mountainous in relief.* | *La Corse a un relief rocheux.* |
| sand | **le sable** |
| shore | **le rivage** |
| slope | **la pente** |
| surface | **la surface** |
| terrain | **le terrain** |
| terrestrial | **terrestre** |
| valley | **la vallée** |
| volcano | **le volcan** |
| wood | **le bois** |
| wooded | **boisé(e)** |
| *This is a wooded area.* | *C'est un terrain boisé.* |

| | |
|---|---|
| **WATER** | **L'EAU** |
| bank | **la rive/la berge** |
| bay | **la baie** |
| beach | **la plage** |
| brook | **le ruisseau** |
| canal | **le canal** |
| *This canal reaches the sea.* | *Ce canal va jusqu'à la mer.* |
| cascade | **la cascade** |
| channel | **le bras de mer** |

| | |
|---|---|
| confluence | **la confluence** |
| current | **le courant** |
| downstream | **en aval** |
| gulf | **le golfe** |
| isthmus | **l'isthme (m)** |
| lake | **le lac** |
| navigable | **navigable** |
| ocean | **l'océan (m)** |
| pond | **l'étang (m)** |
| *The pond is covered with water lilies.* | ***L'étang est couvert de nénuphars.*** |
| river mouth | **l'embouchure (f)** |
| river | **le fleuve/la rivière** |
| sea | **la mer** |
| source | **la source** |
| tide | **la marée** |
| torrent | **le torrent** |
| tributary | **l'affluent** |
| upstream | **en amont** |
| waterfall | **la chute d'eau** |
| wave | **la vague** |
| *The waves are high.* | ***Les vagues sont hautes.*** |

| **COORDINATES** | **COORDONNÉES** |
|---|---|
| compass | **la boussole** |
| east | **l'est (m)** |
| eastern | **oriental(e)** |
| latitude | **la latitude** |
| longitude | **la longitude** |
| meridian | **le méridien** |
| north | **le nord** |
| northern | **septentrional(e)** |
| south | **le sud** |
| southern | **méridional(e)** |
| west | **l'ouest (m)** |
| western | **occidental(e)** |

# Weather and Seasons

## Weather Conditions

| | |
|---|---|
| The weather is bad. | *Il fait mauvais.* |
| The weather is cloudy. | *Il fait nuageux.* |
| The weather is cold. | *Il fait froid.* |
| The weather is cool. | *Il fait frais.* |
| The weather is foggy. | *Il fait du brouillard.* |
| The weather is gray. | *Il fait gris/maussade.* |
| The weather is hot. | *Il fait chaud.* |
| The weather is humid. | *Il fait humide/lourd.* |
| The weather is mild. | *Il fait doux.* |
| The weather is nice. | *Il fait beau/bon.* |
| The weather is rainy. | *Il fait pluvieux.* |
| The weather is stormy. | *Il fait orageux.* |
| The weather is sunny. | *Il fait du soleil.* |
| The weather is windy. | *Il fait du vent.* |

## Conditions atmosphériques

 **Must-Know Tip**

Remember that most weather expressions start with "**Il fait...**" meaning "*The weather is . . . ,*" except for "**Il neige, Il gèle, Il pleut, Il grêle.**"

| | |
|---|---|
| It is snowing. | *Il neige.* |
| It is freezing. | *Il gèle.* |
| It is hailing. | *Il grêle.* |
| It is raining. | *Il pleut.* |
| It is raining in torrents. | *Il pleut à torrents.* |

 **Must-Know Tip**

Watch for the different ways to describe rain. They cannot always be translated literally. For example, "**Il pleut à verse**" means *It is pouring rain*; "**Il pleut des cordes**" is the equivalent of "*It is raining cats and dogs.*"

| | |
|---|---|
| break/clear up | s'éclaircir |
| break in the weather | l'éclaircie (f) |
| *We are waiting for a break in the rain to go out.* | *Nous attendons une éclaircie pour sortir.* |
| breeze | la brise |
| dry | sec/sèche |
| fog | le brouillard |
| frost | le gel/le givre |
| hail | la grêle |
| heat | la chaleur |
| ice | la glace/le gel/le verglas |
| *A car can easily skid on ice.* | *Une voiture peut facilement déraper sur le verglas.* |
| mist | la brume |
| overcast | couvert(e) |
| *The sky is cloudy. It is going to rain.* | *Le ciel est couvert. Il va pleuvoir.* |
| rain | la pluie |
| rainbow | l'arc-en-ciel (m) |
| shower, rain shower | l'averse (f) |
| snow | la neige |
| sun | le soleil |
| sunny | ensoleillé(e) |
| *The South of France is sunny today.* | *Le Midi de la France est ensoleillé aujourd'hui.* |
| thaw | le dégel |
| *torrential rain* | *une pluie diluvienne* |
| wind | le vent |

 **Must-Know Tip**

Watch out for weather expressions referring to animals such as "**Il fait un froid de canard,**" which means that it is really cold or "**Il fait un temps de chien,**" which means that the weather is bad. These cannot be translated literally.

## Extreme Weather Conditions and Natural Disasters

## Conditions atmosphériques sévères et désastres naturels

| | |
|---|---|
| avalanche | l'avalanche (f) |
| cyclone | le cyclone |
| disaster zone | la zone sinistrée |
| dog days | la canicule |
| drought | la sécheresse |
| earthquake | le tremblement de terre |
| eruption | l'éruption (f) |
| flood | l'inondation (f) |
| hurricane | l'ouragan (m) |
| iceberg | l'iceberg (m) |
| landslide | le glissement/l'effondrement de terrain (m) |

*The landslide swallowed entire houses.* — *Le glissement de terrain a englouti des maisons entières.*

| | |
|---|---|
| lava | la lave |
| lightning bolt | la foudre |
| lightning | l'éclair (m) |
| monsoon | la mousson |
| seismic | le séisme |
| shock | la secousse |
| snowstorm | la tempête de neige |

*Snowstorms sometimes cause avalanches.* — *Les tempêtes de neige causent parfois des avalanches.*

| | |
|---|---|
| squall | la rafale |
| storm (at sea) | la tempête |
| storm | l'orage (m) |
| thunder | le tonnerre |
| tidal wave | le raz-de-marée |
| tornado | la tornade |
| torrential rains | les pluies torrentielles (fpl) |
| tsunami | le tsunami |
| typhoon | le typhon |
| windstorm | la tempête de vent |

## Weather Report

| | |
|---|---|
| annual | **annuel(le)** |
| atmospheric pressure | **la pression atmosphérique** |
| average | **moyen(ne)** |
| *The temperature is below average.* | *La température est sous la moyenne.* |
| barometer | **le baromètre** |
| change | **le changement** |
| coolness | **la fraîcheur** |
| degree | **le degré** |
| disturbance | **la perturbation** |
| drop | **baisser** |
| forecast | **la prévision** |
| high pressure | **la haute pression** |
| hit hard | **taper/frapper fort** |
| *The sun hits hard.* | *Le soleil tape fort.* |
| in the shade | **à l'ombre** |
| low pressure | **la basse pression** |
| mildness | **la douceur** |
| minus | **moins** |
| plus | **plus** |
| precipitation | **la précipitation** |
| rise | **monter** |
| shine | **briller** |
| sunrise | **le lever du soleil** |
| sunset | **le coucher du soleil** |
| *What a spectacular sunset!* | *Quel coucher de soleil spectaculaire!* |
| temperature | **la température** |
| thermometer | **le thermomètre** |
| variable | **variable** |

## Seasons  —  **Les saisons**

| | |
|---|---|
| fall | **l'automne (m)** |
| spring | **le printemps** |
| summer | **l'été (m)** |

| winter | l'hiver (m) |
| In the wintertime, I go skiing in Québec. | L'hiver je fais du ski au Québec. |

 **Must-Know Tip**

Remember to express *in the winter, in the summer, in the fall,* and *in the spring* as **en hiver** or **l'hiver, en été** or **l'été, en automne** or **l'automne,** and **au printemps** or **le printemps.**

## Climates — Les climats

| Climates | Les climats |
| --- | --- |
| aurora borealis | l'aurore boréale (f) |
| continental | continental(e) |
| Mediterranean | méditerranéen(ne) |
| polar | polaire |
| temperate | tempéré(e) |
| tropical | tropical(e) |
| zone | la zone |

# Ecology and Pollution

## Ecology — L'écologie

| Ecology | L'écologie |
| --- | --- |
| biological | biologique |
| demand | revendiquer |
| diversity | la diversité |
| *Ecologists want to preserve biological diversity.* | *Les écologistes veulent préserver la diversité biologique.* |
| Earth | la terre |
| ecologist | l'écologiste (m/f) |
| ecosystem | l'écosystème (m) |
| environmentalist | le défenseur de l'environnement |

| | |
|---|---|
| fauna | **la faune** |
| flora | **la flore** |
| global | **planétaire** |
| habitat | **l'habitat (m)** |
| imbalance | **le déséquilibre** |
| irreversible | **irréversible** |
| natural resources | **les ressources naturelles (fpl)** |
| ozone layer | **la couche d'ozone** |
| *There is a hole in the ozone layer.* | *Il y a un trou dans la couche d'ozone.* |
| preserve | **préserver** |
| protect | **protéger/sauvegarder** |
| protection | **la protection/la sauvegarde** |
| recycle | **recycler** |
| recycling | **le recyclage** |
| species | **l'espèce (f)** |
| wilderness | **la nature sauvage** |

## Pollution

## La pollution

| | |
|---|---|
| acid rain | **les pluies acides (fpl)** |
| allergy | **l'allergie (f)** |
| Amazon rainforest | **la forêt amazonienne** |
| atomic | **atomique** |
| biodegradable | **biodégradable** |
| block/stop | **enrayer** |
| *We must stop deforestation.* | *Il faut enrayer le déboisement.* |
| burn | **la brûlure** |
| cancer | **le cancer** |
| carbon dioxide | **le dioxide de carbone ($CO_2$)** |
| cell mutation | **la mutation de cellules** |
| chemical | **chimique** |
| cleanup | **le nettoyage** |
| concern | **l'inquiétude (f)** |
| contamination | **la contamination** |
| *The contamination of ocean waters kills fish.* | *La contamination des eaux de l'océan tue le poisson.* |

| | |
|---|---|
| coral reef | **le récif de corail** |
| damage | **abîmer** |
| damage | **le dégât** |
| deforestation | **le déboisement** |
| degradation | **la dégradation** |
| desertification | **la désertification** |
| destruction | **la destruction** |
| disappear | **disparaître** |
| drinking water | **l'eau potable** |
| *Chemical waste seeps into drinking water.* | *Les déchets chimiques s'infiltrent dans l'eau potable.* |
| dump | **décharger** |
| dump | **la décharge** |
| erode | **s'éroder** |
| erosion | **l'érosion (f)** |
| extinction | **la disparition** |
| fertilizer | **l'engrais (m)** |
| flood | **l'inondation (f)** |
| garbage | **les ordures (fpl)** |
| garbage can | **la poubelle** |
| gas | **le gaz** |
| greenhouse effect | **l'effet de serre (m)** |
| harmful | **nocif/nocive** |
| hole | **le trou** |
| ice cap | **la calotte glaciaire** |
| *The Antarctic ice cap is melting.* | *La calotte glaciaire de l'Antarctique est en train de fondre.* |
| ice sheet | **la plate-forme glaciaire** |
| illness | **la maladie** |
| impact | **l'impact (m)** |
| *in danger of extinction* | *en voie de disparition* |
| index | **l'indice (m)** |
| industrial | **industriel(le)** |
| industrialization | **l'industrialisation (f)** |

| | |
|---|---|
| inexorable | **inexorable** |
| invade | **envahir** |
| melanoma | **le mélanome** |
| melt | **fondre** |
| nuclear | **nucléaire** |
| oil | **le pétrole** |
| oil slick | **la marée noire** |
| *Oil slicks cause the death of fish and birds.* | ***Les marées noires causent la mort des poissons et des oiseaux.*** |
| oil tanker | **le pétrolier** |
| ozone shield | **le bouclier d'ozone** |
| plankton | **le plancton** |
| poaching | **le braconnage** |
| pollutant | **le polluant** |
| pollute | **polluer** |
| polluter | **le pollueur/la pollueuse** |
| pollution control | **la maîtrise de la pollution** |
| power plant | **la centrale** |
| radioactive | **radioactif(-ve)** |
| *Radioactive emissions cause inexorable damage.* | ***Les émissions radioactives causent des dégâts inexorables.*** |
| regress | **reculer** |
| respiratory | **respiratoire** |
| rise | **la montée/l'augmentation** |
| rise | **monter/augmenter** |
| site | **le site** |
| spilled | **répandu(e)** |
| storage | **le stockage** |
| stratosphere | **la stratosphère** |
| sunburn | **le coup de soleil** |
| *Sunburns age your skin.* | ***Les coups de soleil vieillissent la peau.*** |
| sunstroke | **l'insolation (f)** |
| tear | **la fissure** |
| threat | **la menace** |

| | |
|---|---|
| threshold | **le seuil** |
| toxic | **toxique** |
| treatment | **le traitement** |
| ultraviolet rays | **les rayons ultraviolets (mpl)** |
| urban development | **l'urbanisation (f)** |
| *Urban development hurts animal habitat.* | ***L'urbanisation nuit à l'habitat animal.*** |
| warming | **le réchauffement** |
| waste | **gaspiller** |
| waste | **le gaspillage** |
| waste/garbage | **les déchêts** |
| water level | **le niveau de l'eau** |
| wildlife | **les animaux sauvages (mpl)** |

# Farms and Gardens

## Agriculture and Farming

## L'agriculture et l'élevage

| | |
|---|---|
| agricultural | **agricole** |
| agriculture | **l'agriculture (f)** |
| agriculturist | **l'agriculteur/l'agricultrice** |
| arable | **arable** |
| *All arable land is cultivated.* | ***Toutes les terres arables sont cultivées.*** |
| breed/raise | **élever** |
| breeder | **l'éleveur (m)** |
| breeding/raising | **l'élevage (m)** |
| cattle | **le bétail** |
| country | **la campagne** |
| country-style/rural | **campagnard(e)** |
| cultivate/grow | **cultiver** |
| cultivation | **la culture** |
| early vegetables and fruits | **les primeurs** |
| farmer | **le fermier/la fermière** |
| farmer/peasant | **le cultivateur/la cultivatrice** |
| *This farmer produces corn.* | ***Ce cultivateur produit du maïs.*** |

| | |
|---|---|
| fertile | **fertile** |
| field | **le champ** |
| fish farming | **la pisciculture** |
| forest | **la forêt** |
| fungicide | **le fongicide** |
| grape harvest | **la vendange** |
| harvest grapes | **vendanger** |
| harvest | **la récolte/la moisson** |
| harvest | **récolter/moissonner** |
| horticulture | **l'horticulture (f)** |
| market gardening | **la culture maraîchère** |
| meadow | **le pré** |
| *Cows graze in the meadows.* | *Les vaches paissent dans les prés.* |
| moisture | **l'humidité (f)** |
| organic gardening | **le jardinage biologique** |
| pasture | **le pâturage** |
| shade | **l'ombre (f)** |
| soil | **la terre** |
| sow | **semer** |
| sunlight | **la lumière du soleil** |
| vineyard | **le vignoble** |
| viticulturist | **le viticulteur/la viticultrice** |
| wine | **le vin** |
| winegrower | **le/la vigneron(ne)** |
| winegrowing | **viticole** |
| *The winegrowing industry is important in this region.* | *L'industrie viticole est importante dans cette région.* |
| yield | **le rendement** |
| yield | **rendre** |

## Farming and Gardening Tools

## Les outils du cultivateur et du jardinier

| | |
|---|---|
| barrel | **le tonneau** |
| equipment | **l'équipement (m)** |
| gloves | **les gants (mpl)** |

| | |
|---|---|
| insecticide | l'insecticide (m) |
| manure/fertilizer | l'engrais (m) |
| pesticide | le pesticide |
| plow | la charrue |
| pruner | le sécateur |
| *I need shears to trim my rose tree.* | *J'ai besoin d'un sécateur pour tailler mon rosier.* |
| rake | le rateau |
| shovel | la pelle |
| spray | asperger/vaporiser |
| sprinkler system | l'arrosage automatique (m) |
| sprinkler | le jet d'eau |
| tractor | le tracteur |
| truck | le camion |
| watering can | l'arrosoir (m) |
| watering hose | le tuyau d'arrosage |
| weed killer | le désherbant (m) |
| *We should put weed killer on this lawn.* | *Il faudrait mettre du désherbant sur ce gazon.* |
| wheelbarrow | la brouette |

## Fruit, Fruit Trees, and Grain

## Fruits, arbres fruitiers et grains

| | |
|---|---|
| **FRUIT AND FRUIT TREES** | **LES FRUITS ET LES ARBRES FRUITIERS** |
| almond | l'amande (f) |
| almond tree | l'amandier (m) |
| apple | la pomme |
| apple tree | le pommier |
| apricot | l'abricot (m) |
| apricot tree | l'abricotier (m) |
| avocado | l'avocat (m) |
| avocado tree | l'avocatier (m) |
| banana | la banane |
| banana tree | le bananier |

| | |
|---|---|
| cherry | **la cerise** |
| cherry tree | **le cerisier** |
| fig | **la figue** |
| fig tree | **le figuier** |
| grapefruit | **le pamplemousse** |
| grapefruit tree | **le pamplemoussier** |
| lemon | **le citron** |
| lemon tree | **le citronnier** |
| mandarin | **la mandarine** |
| mandarin tree | **le mandarinier** |
| mango | **la mangue** |
| mango tree | **le manguier** |
| olive | **l'olive (f)** |
| olive tree | **l'olivier (m)** |
| *In Provence, there are many olive trees.* | ***En Provence il y a beaucoup d'oliviers.*** |
| orange | **l'orange (f)** |
| orange tree | **l'oranger (m)** |
| peach | **la pêche** |
| peach tree | **le pêcher** |
| pear | **la poire** |
| pear tree | **le poirier** |
| plum | **la prune** |
| plum tree | **le prunier** |

 **Must-Know Tip**

Remember that most fruit (except for **abricot**, **avocat**, **citron**, **pamplemousse**) have the feminine gender (**la prune**), while fruit trees always have the masculine gender (**le prunier**).

| **GRAIN** | **LE GRAIN** |
|---|---|
| barley | **l'orge (f)** |
| cereal | **la céréale** |

| | |
|---|---|
| corn | le maïs |
| oats | l'avoine (f) |
| rye | le seigle |
| wheat | le blé/le froment |
| *I love whole wheat bread.* | *J'adore le pain de froment.* |

## Flowers, Shrubs, and Trees

## Les fleurs, les arbustes et les arbres

### FLOWERS AND SHRUBS

### LES FLEURS ET LES ARBUSTES

| | |
|---|---|
| annual | la plante annuelle |
| bloom | fleurir |
| bud | le bouton |
| bulb | la bulbe |
| carnation | l'œillet (m) |
| cut | couper |
| daffodil | la jonquille |
| daisy | la pâquerette/la marguerite |
| *He is pushing up the daisies.* | *Il est mort et enterré.* |
| gladiolus | le glaïeul |
| grow | pousser |
| heather | la bruyère |
| hedge | la haie |
| hydrangea | l'hortensia (m) |
| ivy | le lierre |
| lilac | le lilas |
| lily of the valley | le muguet |
| *On the first of May, everybody looks for lilies of the valley.* | *Le premier mai, tout le monde cherche du muguet.* |
| lily | le lys |
| orchid | l'orchidée (f) |
| perennial | la vivace |
| plant | la plante |
| plant | planter |
| poppy | le coquelicot |

| | |
|---|---|
| rose tree, rose bush | **le rosier** |
| sunflower | **le tournesol** |
| trim | **tailler** |
| tulip | **la tulipe** |
| *I will replant my tulip bulbs next winter.* | *Je replanterai mes bulbes de tulipe l'hiver prochain.* |
| violet | **la violette** |
| weed | **la mauvaise herbe** |

**TREES**

**LES ARBRES**

| | |
|---|---|
| beech | **le hêtre** |
| birch | **le bouleau** |
| elm | **l'orme (m)** |
| fir | **le sapin** |
| linden tree | **le tilleul** |
| *A blooming linden tree smells good.* | *Un tilleul en fleur sent bon.* |
| maple | **l'érable (m)** |
| oak | **le chêne** |
| palm tree | **le palmier** |
| pine | **le pin** |
| plane tree | **le platane** |
| poplar | **le peuplier** |
| willow | **le saule** |
| *weeping willow* | *le saule pleureur* |

# Pets and Animals

## Pets

## Les bêtes

| | |
|---|---|
| cat | **le chat/la chatte** |
| *Cats purr.* | *Les chats ronronnent.* |
| chinchilla | **le chinchilla** |
| dog | **le chien/la chienne** |
| domestic animal | **l'animal domestique (m)** |
| frog | **la grenouille** |

| | |
|---|---|
| goldfish | **le poisson rouge** |
| hamster | **le hamster** |
| lizard | **le lézard** |
| parrot | **le perroquet** |
| rabbit | **le lapin** |
| tortoise | **la tortue** |

## Farm and Field Animals

## Les animaux de la ferme et des champs

| | |
|---|---|
| bat | **la chauve-souris** |
| bull | **le taureau** |
| calf | **le veau** |
| chick | **le poussin** |
| *The hen had ten chicks.* | *La poule a eu dix poussins.* |
| chicken coop | **le poulailler** |
| cow | **la vache** |
| donkey | **l'âne/l'ânesse** |
| dormouse | **le loir** |
| duck | **le canard** |
| duckling | **le caneton** |
| ewe | **la brebis** |
| farmyard | **la basse-cour** |
| field mouse | **le mulot** |
| goat | **la chèvre** |
| *France produces good goat cheese.* | *La France produit de bons fromages de chèvre.* |
| goose | **l'oie (f)** |
| guinea pig | **le cochon d'Inde** |
| hare | **le lièvre** |
| hen | **la poule** |
| herd | **le troupeau** |
| horse | **le cheval** |
| lamb | **l'agneau (m)** |
| mare | **la jument** |

| marmot | la marmotte |
| mole | la taupe |
| *A mole is digging holes in my garden.* | *Une taupe creuse des trous dans mon jardin.* |
| mouse | la souris |
| mule | la mule |
| ox | le bœuf |
| pig | le cochon |
| pony | le poney |
| porcupine | le porc-épic |
| poultry | la volaille |
| rabbit | le lapin |
| raccoon | le raton laveur |
| ram | le bélier |
| *This ram has big horns.* | *Ce bélier a de grandes cornes.* |
| rat | le rat/la ratte |
| rooster | le coq |
| sheep | le mouton |
| sow | la truie |
| squirrel | l'écureuil (m) |
| stallion | l'étalon (m) |
| swan | le cygne |
| turkey | la dinde |

## African Animals — Les animaux africains

| antelope | l'antilope (f) |
| boa | le boa |
| crocodile | le crocodile |
| elephant | l'éléphant (m) |
| giraffe | la girafe |
| gorilla | le gorille |
| hippopotamus | l'hippopotame (m) |
| *The hippopotamus loves water.* | *L'hippopotame adore l'eau.* |
| hyena | l'hyène (f) |

| | |
|---|---|
| jackal | le chacal |
| leopard | le léopard/la léoparde |
| lion | le lion/la lionne |
| monkey | le singe |
| ostrich | l'autruche (f) |
| rhinoceros | le rhinocéros |
| snake | le serpent |
| tiger | le tigre/la tigresse |
| vulture | le vautour |
| *The vulture is a bird of prey.* | *Le vautour est un oiseau rapace.* |
| wild animal | le fauve |
| zebra | le zèbre |

## Endangered Species / Les espèces en danger

| | |
|---|---|
| armadillo | l'armadillo (m) |
| bear | l'ours (m) |
| butterfly | le papillon |
| cheetah | le guépard |
| chimpanzee | le chimpanzé |
| cougar | le cougar |
| dolphin | le dauphin |
| *Some types of dolphin are endangered species.* | *Certains types de dauphins sont des espèces en danger.* |
| gorilla | le gorille |
| ibis | l'ibis (m) |
| jaguar | le jaguar |
| koala | le koala |
| leopard | le léopard |
| lynx | le lynx |
| panther | la panthère |
| *Panthers live in the savannah.* | *Les panthères vivent dans la savane.* |
| pelican | le pélican |
| penguin | le pingouin |
| porpoise | le marsouin |

| | |
|---|---|
| rhinoceros | **le rhinocéros** |
| seal | **le phoque** |
| shark | **le requin** |
| skunk | **la moufette** |
| turtle | **la tortue** |
| whale | **la baleine** |
| wolf | **le loup** |
| *Wolves have been relocated.* | *Les loups ont été déplacés.* |

## Birds — Les oiseaux

| | |
|---|---|
| blackbird | **le merle** |
| cardinal | **le cardinal** |
| condor | **le condor** |
| dove | **la colombe** |
| eagle | **l'aigle (m)** |
| flamingo | **le flamand** |
| lark | **l'alouette (f)** |
| magpie | **la pie** |

### Must-Know Tip

Be aware that there are numerous expressions comparing people to animals such as "**voleur comme une pie,**" which means *"thievish like a magpie"* or "**dormir comme un loir,**" which means *"to sleep like a dormouse."* These cannot always be translated literally.

| | |
|---|---|
| nightingale | **le rossignol** |
| *He sings like a nightingale.* | *Il chante comme un rossignol.* |
| partridge | **la perdrix** |
| pelican | **le pélican** |
| pheasant | **le faisan** |
| pigeon | **le pigeon** |
| seagull | **la mouette** |
| sparrow | **le moineau** |

| | |
|---|---|
| stork | **la cigogne** |
| *You can once again see storks in Alsace.* | *On revoit les cigognes en Alsace.* |
| swallow | **l'hirondelle (f)** |
| titmouse | **la mésange** |
| toucan | **le toucan** |
| turtledove | **le tourtereau/la tourterelle** |

## Insects      Les insectes

| | |
|---|---|
| ant | **la fourmi** |
| bee | **l'abeille (f)** |
| butterfly | **le papillon** |
| cricket | **le criquet** |
| dragonfly | **la libellule** |
| flea | **la puce** |
| fly | **la mouche** |
| locust | **la cigale** |
| mite | **la mite** |
| mosquito | **le moustique** |
| roach | **le cafard** |
| spider | **l'araignée (f)** |
| wasp | **la guêpe** |

# 12

# *Measures, Numbers, and Time*

# Measurements and Quantities

| Measurements | Les mesures |
|---|---|
| size | **la taille** |
| small | **petit(e)** |
| large | **grand(e)** |
| minute | **minuscule** |
| enormous | **énorme** |
| gigantic | **gigantesque** |
| length | **la longueur** |
| long | **long/longue** |
| short | **court(e)** |
| width | **la largeur** |
| wide | **large** |
| *Paris has many beautiful and wide avenues.* | *Paris a beaucoup d'avenues belles et larges.* |
| height | **la hauteur/la grandeur** |
| high | **haut(e)/grand(e)** |
| low | **bas(se)** |
| depth | **la profondeur** |
| deep | **profond(e)** |
| millimeter | **le millimètre** |
| centimeter | **le centimètre** |
| meter | **le mètre** |
| kilometer | **le kilomètre** |
| weight | **le poids** |
| *The postage rate depends on the weight of the envelope.* | *Le tarif du service postal dépend du poids de l'enveloppe.* |
| weigh | **peser** |
| scale | **la balance** |
| heavy | **lourd(e)** |
| light | **léger/légère** |
| surface | **la surface/la superficie** |
| square meter | **le mètre carré** |

| volume | le volume |
| content | le contenu |

## Quantities / Les quantités

| **APPROXIMATIONS** | **APPROXIMATIONS** |
|---|---|
| about ten | une dizaine |
| about twelve | une douzaine |
| about fifteen | une quinzaine |
| about twenty | une vingtaine |
| about thirty | une trentaine |
| about forty | une quarantaine |
| about fifty | une cinquantaine |
| about sixty | une soixantaine |
| *He is about sixty.* | *Il a la soixantaine.* |
| about one hundred | une centaine |
| about one thousand | un millier |

| **NOUNS OF QUANTITY** | **NOMS QUANTITATIFS** |
|---|---|
| bottle | la bouteille |
| box | la boîte |
| cup | la tasse |
| double | le double |
| fourth | le quart |
| glass | le verre |
| gram | le gramme |
| half | la moitié |
| *You only drank half of your milk.* | *Tu n'as bu que la moitié de ton lait.* |
| handful | la poignée |
| kilogram | le kilogramme |
| liter | le litre |
| mouthful | la bouchée |
| pair | la paire |
| percent | pour cent |
| percentage | le pourcentage |
| piece | le morceau |

| | |
|---|---|
| pinch | **la pincée** |
| *Add a pinch of salt!* | *Ajoute une pincée de sel!* |
| pound | **la livre** |
| slice | **la tranche** |
| spoonful | **la cuillerée** |
| third | **le tiers** |
| ton | **la tonne** |
| triple | **le triple** |

| ADVERBS AND ADJECTIVES OF QUANTITY | LES ADVERBES ET ADJECTIFS DE QUANTITÉ |
|---|---|
| a few | **quelques** |
| a little | **un peu (de)** |
| a lot, much, many | **beaucoup (de)/bien du (de la, de l', des)** |
| *We saw each other again after many years.* | *Nous nous sommes revus après bien des années.* |
| as many, as much | **autant (de)** |
| enough | **assez (de)** |
| few | **peu (de)** |
| how many (exclamation) | **que de** |
| *How many mistakes!* | *Que de fautes!* |
| less | **moins (de)** |
| little | **peu (de)** |
| more | **plus (de)** |
| most | **la plupart (du/de la/de l'/des)** |
| several | **plusieurs** |
| so many, so much | **tant (de)** |
| some | **du, de la, de l', des** |
| too many, much | **trop (de)** |

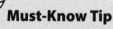 **Must-Know Tip**

When using adverbs of quantity, remember that the preposition **de** remains invariable except in expressions using **bien** and **la plupart**.

# Numbers and Calculations

| Cardinal and Ordinal Numbers | Les nombres cardinaux et ordinaux |
|---|---|
| 0 | **zéro** |
| 1 | **un(e)** |
| 1st | **premier/première** |
| *Today's date is the first of May.* | ***La date d'aujourd'hui est le premier mai.*** |

 **Must-Know Tip**

Remember to use cardinal numbers with dates as in **le 3 mai**, except for the first of each month, which is **le premier**.

| | |
|---|---|
| 2 | **deux** |
| 2nd | **deuxième** |
| 3 | **trois** |
| 3rd | **troisième** |
| 4 | **quatre** |
| 4th | **quatrième** |
| *Henry the Fourth was assassinated.* | ***Henri Quatre a été assassiné.*** |

 **Must-Know Tip**

Remember to use cardinal numbers with names of rulers except for Francis the **First**; use François **Premier**.

| | |
|---|---|
| 5 | **cinq** |
| 5th | **cinquième** |
| 6 | **six** |
| 6th | **sixième** |
| 7 | **sept** |

| | |
|---|---|
| 7th | **septième** |
| 8 | **huit** |
| 8th | **huitième** |
| 9 | **neuf** |
| 9th | **neuvième** |
| 10 | **dix** |
| 10th | **dixième** |
| 11 | **onze** |
| 11th | **onzième** |
| 12 | **douze** |
| 12th | **douzième** |
| 13 | **treize** |
| 13th | **treizième** |
| 14 | **quatorze** |
| 14th | **quatorzième** |
| 15 | **quinze** |
| 15th | **quinzième** |
| 16 | **seize** |
| 16th | **seizième** |
| 17 | **dix-sept** |
| 17th | **dix-septième** |
| 18 | **dix-huit** |
| 18th | **dix-huitième** |
| 19 | **dix-neuf** |
| 19th | **dix-neuvième** |
| 20 | **vingt** |
| 20th | **vingtième** |
| 21 | **vingt et un(e)** |
| 21st | **vingt et unième** |
| 22 | **vingt-deux** |
| 22nd | **vingt-deuxième** |
| 30 | **trente** |
| 30th | **trentième** |
| 40 | **quarante** |
| 40th | **quarantième** |

| | |
|---|---|
| 50 | **cinquante** |
| 50th | **cinquantième** |
| 60 | **soixante** |
| 60th | **soixantième** |
| 70 | **soixante-dix** |
| 70th | **soixante-dixième** |
| 80 | **quatre-vingts** |
| 80th | **quatre-vingtième** |
| 90 | **quatre-vingt-dix** |
| 90th | **quatre-vingt-dixième** |
| 100 | **cent** |
| 100th | **centième** |
| 110 | **cent dix** |
| 110th | **cent dixième** |
| 200 | **deux cents** |
| 200th | **deux centième** |
| 210 | **deux cent dix** |
| 210th | **deux cent dixième** |
| 1,000 | **mille** |
| 1,000th | **millième** |
| 2,000 | **deux mille** |
| 2,000th | **deux millième** |
| one million | **un million** |
| one billion | **un milliard** |
| *The lucky lottery winner receives a million Euros.* | ***L'heureux gagnant de la Loterie reçoit un million d'euros.*** |

## Calculations

## Les calculs

| | |
|---|---|
| add | **additionner** |
| addition | **l'addition (f)** |
| calculate | **calculer** |
| count | **compter** |
| difference | **la différence** |
| divide | **diviser** |
| division | **la division** |

| | |
|---|---|
| multiplication | **la multiplication** |
| *three times three equals nine* | ***trois fois trois font neuf*** |
| number | **le chiffre/le nombre/le numéro** |
| *There are seven digits in my phone number.* | ***Il y a sept chiffres dans mon numéro de téléphone.*** |

 **Must-Know Tip**

Remember to use the appropriate word for number. **Le chiffre** is used for a figure or a digit; **le numéro** is used for a whole number such as in a street address or a phone number; **le nombre** is used in counting.

| | |
|---|---|
| subtract | **soustraire** |
| subtraction | **la soustraction** |
| *five minus two is three* | ***cinq moins deux font trois*** |
| sum | **la somme** |
| total | **le total** |

# Time, Days, and Months

## Time

## L'heure

| | |
|---|---|
| What time is it? | **Quelle heure est-il?** |
| Do you have the time? | **Vous avez l'heure?** |
| At what time does the bank open? | **À quelle heure ouvre la banque?** |
| *It is 4:15 A.M.* | ***Il est quatre heures quinze du matin.*** |
| *until 2:50* | ***jusqu'à deux heures cinquante*** |
| *starting at 3:10* | ***à partir de trois heures dix*** |
| *5:15 P.M.* | ***cinq heures et quart de l'après-midi*** |
| *6:30 P.M.* | ***six heures et demie du soir*** |
| *7:40* | ***huit heures moins vingt*** |
| *8:45* | ***neuf heures moins le quart*** |
| *at exactly 1 P.M.* | ***à treize heures précises*** |

| | |
|---|---|
| noon | **midi** |
| midnight | **minuit** |
| day | **le jour** |
| morning | **le matin** |
| afternoon | **l'après-midi (m/f)** |
| evening | **le soir** |
| night | **la nuit** |
| *I sleep during the daytime and party at night.* | *Je dors le jour et je fais la fête la nuit.* |

## Days

## Les jours

| | |
|---|---|
| Monday | **lundi** |
| Tuesday | **mardi** |
| Wednesday | **mercredi** |
| Thursday | **jeudi** |
| Friday | **vendredi** |
| Saturday | **samedi** |
| Sunday | **dimanche** |
| *On Sundays, I usually rest but next Sunday I have to work.* | *Le dimanche, je me repose d'habitude, mais dimanche prochain je dois travailler.* |

## Months

| Months | Les mois |
|---|---|
| January | janvier |
| *He was born on January 30, 1971.* | *Il est né le 30 janvier 1971.* |
| February | février |
| March | mars |
| April | avril |
| May | mai |
| June | juin |
| July | juillet |
| August | août |
| September | septembre |
| October | octobre |
| November | novembre |
| December | décembre |
| *The month of December is my favorite month.* | *Le mois de décembre est mon mois préféré.* |

# Exercises

The exercises that follow correspond to the units in this book. Exercise 5.2, for example, refers to vocabulary you encountered in Unit 5. As in the rest of the book, the exercises are set up so you can focus on any subject area that interests you, such as shopping in Unit 5, and move from one unit to another. Enjoy your practice!

## 1.1

*Quelques données personnelles.* Choose the correct meaning for each French sentence.

| | |
|---|---|
| 1. Je suis étudiant. | a. Her last name is American. |
| 2. Ma sœur est pharmacienne. | b. We live in the same area. |
| 3. Elle est mariée à un Américain. | c. I am a student. |
| 4. Son nom de famille est américain. | d. She is married to an American. |
| 5. Nous habitons dans le même quartier. | e. My sister is a pharmacist. |

## 1.2

*Une conversation téléphonique.* Put the following sentences in chronological order (from 1 to 8) to create a telephone conversation.

_____ 1. Je regrette, mademoiselle. Il y a erreur.

_____ 2. Ah! Vous êtes l'amie de mon fils François. Le voilà!

_____ 3. De rien, mademoiselle. Au revoir.

_____ 4. Mais vous avez le mauvais numéro.

_____ 5. Ne quittez pas, s'il vous plaît, madame.

_____ 6. Allô. C'est Mireille à l'appareil.

_____ 7. Permettez-moi de me présenter; c'est Mireille Lajoie.

_____ 8. Merci, madame. Au revoir.

## 1.3

*Le courrier et les visites.* Indicate True (*Vrai*) or False (*Faux*) for each sentence.

_____ 1. L'adresse comprend le code postal.

_____ 2. L'expéditeur est la personne qui reçoit le courrier.

_____ 3. Le destinataire est la personne qui envoie la lettre.

_____ 4. Le courriel est plus rapide qu'une lettre postale.

_____ 5. Le mot de passe ne permet pas accès à Internet.

_____ 6. On peut télécharger un texte d'Internet quand on est connecté.

_____ 7. L'hôtesse accepte volontiers un cadeau.

_____ 8. L'invité offre des fleurs à l'hôtesse.

_____ 9. On envoie des faire-part ou des invitations à la famille pour un mariage.

_____ 10. Il y a toujours un cocktail à l'église ou au temple.

## 1.4

_Les notions de temps._ Complete each sentence with the correct word.

1. Janvier est le _____ de l'année.

2. Le _____ , c'est une fête et un jour férié.

3. La banque ouvre à huit heures _____.

4. La poste ferme à cinq heures _____.

5. On travaille tous les jours excepté _____.

6. Quelle _____ est-il? Trois heures précises.

7. Ces étudiants travaillent jour et _____.

8. La pharmacie reste ouverte _____ heures sur 24.

a. nuit

b. le samedi et le dimanche

c. du matin

d. heure

e. 24

f. du soir

g. premier mai

h. premier mois

## 1.5

*Les invitations.* With a check mark, indicate what is likely to happen if you are invited to a party you would definitely like to attend.

_____ 1. J'achète une carte de vœux.

_____ 2. Je dis: "Je suis désolé(e) de ne pas pouvoir venir."

_____ 3. J'accepte avec plaisir.

_____ 4. J'achète une montre.

_____ 5. Je reçois une invitation.

## 1.6

*Les adverbes.* Circle the appropriate English translation for each of the following words.

| | | | | |
|---|---|---|---|---|
| 1. already | a. jamais | b. déjà | c. demain | d. aujourd' hui |
| 2. better | a. moins | b. mieux | c. pire | d. bien |
| 3. from time to time | a. maintenant | b. à temps | c. rarement | d. de temps en temps |
| 4. never | a. souvent | b. jamais | c. maintenant | d. plus tard |
| 5. little | a. peu | b. beaucoup | c. moins | d. plus |
| 6. sometimes | a. une fois | b. quelquefois | c. enfin | d. partout |
| 7. enough | a. trop | b. réellement | c. assez | d. vite |
| 8. late | a. à l'heure | b. en retard | c. pressé | d. en avance |
| 9. very | a. très | b. beaucoup | c. si | d. bien |
| 10. soon | a. avant | b. tout de suite | c. bientôt | d. après |

## 1.7

*Les questions.* Choose the best interrogative word to complete each question.

a. quel     b. Depuis quand     c. Qui     d. Où     e. Que

1. _____ est arrivé le premier?

2. _____ désires-tu?

3. Avec _____ mot de passe est-ce que tu te connectes?

4. _____ est-ce que tu habites ici?

5. _____ est-ce que tu vas?

## 1.8

*Les pronoms.* Each sentence in this e-mail written by Sandrine is missing a pronoun. Complete the message by circling the correct answer from the two choices in italics.

1. Mon nom est Sandrine. Quel est le *mien/tien*?
2. Moi, j'adore communiquer par e-mail. Et *toi/lui*?
3. Mes amis *me/te* parlent tous les jours au téléphone.
4. Et les *tiens/tiennes*, ils t'appellent tous les jours aussi?
5. On peut se rencontrer un samedi ou un dimanche. *Quel/Lequel* de ces deux jours préfères-tu?

## 2.1

*La description.* Choose the correct meaning for each sentence.

| | | |
|---|---|---|
| _____ 1. J'ai un nez en trompette. | a. Dogs are very faithful. |
| _____ 2. Je suis mince mais musclé. | b. Children are playful by nature. |
| _____ 3. J'ai les yeux noisette. | c. I have a turned-up nose. |
| _____ 4. Il est roux. Que c'est mignon! | d. Sick people often lack energy. |
| _____ 5. On apprécie les commerçants honnêtes. | e. This baby is plump. |
| _____ 6. Je suis débrouillarde quand il le faut. | f. I am thin but muscular. |
| _____ 7. Les chiens sont très fidèles. | g. He has red hair. How cute! |
| _____ 8. Les malades sont souvent amorphes. | h. I have hazel eyes. |
| _____ 9. Les enfants sont enjoués de nature. | i. We appreciate honest storekeepers. |
| _____ 10. Ce bébé est dodu. | j. I am resourceful when necessary. |

## 2.2

*Le visage.* Choose the most logical completion for each sentence.

| | | |
|---|---|---|
| 1. Paulette a _____ en amande. | a. un physique |
| 2. Son mari a _____ châtains et raides. | b. les lèvres |
| 3. Leur fille a _____ charnues et rouges. | c. les yeux |
| 4. Leur fils a _____ fluet et maigrichon. | d. les cheveux |
| 5. Moi, j'ai _____ bleus et ronds. | |

## 2.3

*La personnalité.* Identify each person's unique personal trait with an appropriate adjective.

1. Ma mère aime créer. Elle est _____.

2. Mon cousin est taciturne et peu sociable. Il est _____.

3. Mon frère n'aime pas attendre. Il est _____.

4. Ma sœur prend des risques. Elle est _____.

5. Mon père ne se fatigue pas d'essayer. Il est _____.

## 2.4

*Les nationalités et les origines.* Choose the best answer for each question.

| | | |
|---|---|---|
| _____ 1. Tu connais le Parthénon à Athènes? | a. Il est originaire de la Tunisie. |
| _____ 2. Tu aimes la cuisine italienne? | b. Oui, surtout les vietnamiens. |
| _____ 3. Quelles montres préfères-tu? | c. Il est délicieux, mais très fort. |
| _____ 4. Quel est le sport canadien par excellence? | d. J'adore la pizza. |
| _____ 5. Comment est le café cubain? | e. À Port-au-Prince. |

_____ 6. Elle te plaît, ma nouvelle
         voiture?

f. Le hockey sur glace!

_____ 7. Où est né ton collègue
         haïtien?

g. Oui, ils vivent à Madrid.

_____ 8. D'où vient cet auteur
         maghrébin?

h. Les meilleures au monde
   sont les Suisses.

_____ 9. Tu as des amis espagnols?

i. Oui, c'est un monument
   grec célèbre.

_____ 10. Les restaurants asiatiques
          sont super, non?

j. Elle est allemande,
   n'est-ce pas?

## 2.5

_Les fêtes._ Indicate True (_Vrai_) or False (_Faux_) for each statement.

_____ 1. La Fête des Mères, c'est toujours en juin.

_____ 2. Pour le Carnaval, on se déguise et on va à des défilés.

_____ 3. En France, la cérémonie officielle du mariage se fait à la mairie.

_____ 4. Pour la St-Valentin, un homme offre des fleurs à sa fiancée.

_____ 5. Seuls les couples mariés fêtent des anniversaires.

## 2.6

_Activités et célébrations familiales._ Circle the appropriate English translation
for each of the following words.

| 1. trust | a. la confiance | b. le bonheur | c. la famille | d. l'amitié |
|---|---|---|---|---|
| 2. quarrel | a. la querelle | b. la chance | c. le groupe | d. la santé |
| 3. birth | a. le baptême | b. la fête | c. la naissance | d. la dispute |
| 4. engagement | a. la lune de miel | b. les fiançailles | c. les noces | d. la tradition |
| 5. gift | a. l'achat | b. l'ami | c. le cadeau | d. la carte |

## 2.7

*Les pays et les langues.* Choose the corresponding question for each answer.

_____ 1. Le portugais, bien sûr!

_____ 2. Dans les Antilles.

_____ 3. Oui, surtout la Chine.

_____ 4. En Amérique du Sud.

_____ 5. En Amérique du Nord.

_____ 6. Arabe et français.

_____ 7. Les Suisses et les Belges.

_____ 8. C'est en Afrique.

a. Quelles langues parle-t-on au Maroc?

b. Sur quel continent est le Sénégal?

c. Où se trouve La Guyane?

d. Où se trouve le Canada?

e. Quels voisins des Français parlent français?

f. Vous connaissez l'Orient?

g. Quelle langue parle-t-on au Brésil?

h. Où se trouve la Martinique?

## 3.1

*Les sens et le corps.* What part of the body is associated with each of the following senses?

_____ 1. le goût

_____ 2. l'ouïe

_____ 3. la vue

_____ 4. le toucher

_____ 5. l'odorat

a. le doigt

b. l'œil

c. le nez

d. la langue

e. l'oreille

## 3.2

*Les parties du corps.* Complete each sentence with an appropriate word from the list.

| | | | | |
|---|---|---|---|---|
| chauve | oignon | ventre | poignet | paupières |
| cils | joue | cou | cheville | coudes |

1. Les femmes se mettent du mascara sur les _____.

2. Je dors avec les _____ fermées.

3. Quand il fait froid, je me couvre le _____ avec une écharpe.

4. Il est _____. Il n'a plus un seul cheveu sur le crâne.

5. En France, les amis s'embrassent sur la _____ pour dire bonjour et au revoir.

6. Elle a trop mangé. Maintenant elle a mal au _____.

7. À force de jouer au tennis, elle a presque toujours mal aux _____.

8. Il a glissé sur une peau de banane et s'est foulé la _____.

9. Je ne peux pas mettre mes sandales à cause de ce vilain _____ sur mon orteil.

10. Je porte trois bracelets au _____ droit.

## 3.3

*L'hygiène.* What activity do you perform with the following objects?

_____ 1. la serviette      a. Je me lave les bras.

_____ 2. le fond de teint      b. Je me nettoie les ongles.

_____ 3. le gant de toilette      c. Je m'essuie après la douche.

_____ 4. la cire épilatoire      d. Je me maquille.

_____ 5. le dissolvant      e. Je m'épile les jambes.

## 3.4

*Sentir, goûter, voir, entendre, toucher.* Write the French word that identifies the sense we use to perceive the following:

1. une boisson froide: _____

2. un repas épicé: _____

3. le fragrance d'une fleur: _____

4. la douceur de la peau: _____

5. la musique rock: _____

6. les couleurs: _____

7. un citron pressé: _____

8. le parfum du thé: _____

9. la sirène de l'ambulance: _____

10. un beau tableau: _____

## 3.5

*Je fais ma toilette.* Translate the following sentences.

1. I gargle. _____

2. I brush my teeth with my new toothbrush. _____

3. I shave with my electric shaver. _____

4. I take a shower. _____

5. My soap smells nice. _____

6. I need a clean towel. _____

7. Oh, no! I do not have deodorant! _____

8. Where are the scissors? _____

9. Now, I am going to trim my mustache. _____

10. And I am going to file my nails. _____

## 3.6

*Une consultation.* Arrange the following sentences in sequence using the letters A through G and create a conversation between a doctor and a patient.

_____ 1. Je sens une grande fatigue et j'ai très mal à la tête.

_____ 2. Qu'est-ce qui ne va pas?

_____ 3. Évidemment. Vous avez une inflammation des amygdales.

_____ 4. Comment allez-vous, madame?

_____ 5. Si, docteur. Je ne peux rien avaler.

_____ 6. Je ne me sens pas bien du tout, docteur.

_____ 7. Vous n'avez pas mal à la gorge?

## 3.7

_Indispositions._ Circle the correct meaning of each French word or expression.

| | | | |
|---|---|---|---|
| 1. se remettre | get sick | get better | get worse |
| 2. somnolence | drowsiness | convalescence | relapse |
| 3. sang | sprain | ache | blood |
| 4. blessure | sneeze | blister | wound |
| 5. douleur | drowsy | pain | colic |
| 6. mal de cœur | queasiness | heartache | sore throat |
| 7. enflé | worse | swollen | hurt |
| 8. faible | weak | fit | feverish |
| 9. grippe | cold | grumpy | flu |
| 10. toux | cough | tonic | sweat |

## 3.8

_Handicaps et remèdes._ Choose the appropriate word for each sentence in the list provided.

diagnostic    paraplégique    repos    symptômes de retrait    caries

myope    oreillons    syrop    sourde-muette    secours

1. Une personne qui ne peut ni entendre ni parler est

   _____ .

2. Une personne qui s'arrête subitement de fumer risque d'avoir des

   _____ .

3. Une personne qui ne peut pas bien voir de loin est

   _____ .

4. Le _____ est basé sur une analyse de sang.

5. Le médecin lui a prescrit un _____ pour la toux.

6. On vaccine les bébés contre les _____ .

7. Après une maladie, il faut du _____.

8. En cas d'accident, il est bon d'avoir un kit de _____.

9. Le _____ est dans une chaise roulante.

10. Un régime qui comporte trop de sucre peut causer des _____ dentaires.

## 3.9

*Les services de santé.* Who is most likely to perform the following services?

1. analyser un électrocardiogramme _____

2. donner une piqûre à un malade _____

3. extraire une dent _____

4. aider à la naissance d'un bébé à domicile _____

5. recommander un régime à un patient _____

6. transporter un patient à l'hôpital _____

7. opérer une appendicite _____

8. faire une auscultation générale _____

9. interpréter une radiographie _____

10. faire des expériences médicales _____

## 3.10

*Le cycle de la vie.* Choose from the list and place the various stages of life in chronological order from birth to death starting with #1 for birth.

| troisième âge | âge de raison | nouveau-né | décédé |
| adolescent | funérailles | majeur | enfant en bas âge |
| adulte | enterrement/incinération | | |

1. _____

2. _____

3. _____

4. _____

5. _____

6. _____

7. _____

8. _____

9. _____

10. _____

## 4.1

*Les établissements scolaires.* Which school does each person attend?

_____ 1. Jacques a trois ans. Il aime colorier.

_____ 2. Ginette sait compter et lire. Elle a sept ans.

_____ 3. Max va avoir son DEUG en juin.

_____ 4. Marie adore ses cours d'hôtellerie. Elle a seize ans.

_____ 5. Raymond enseigne le chant à des petits.

_____ 6. Simone se spécialise en vente et gestion.

_____ 7. Benjamin va être médecin dans deux ans.

_____ 8. Denise qui a neuf ans préfère le travail manuel et le dessin.

a. l'école élémentaire

b. le lycée professionnel

c. la faculté de médecine

d. le jardin d'enfants

e. l'université

## 4.2

*Les étudiants, les cours et les écoles.* Indicate True (*Vrai*) or False (*Faux*) for each sentence.

_____ 1. L'anglais est une matière obligatoire dans les écoles américaines.

_____ 2. Tous les élèves écrivent des livres pour l'école.

_____ 3. Les étudiants qui sèchent les cours vont probablement échouer aux examens.

_____ 4. Les professeurs aiment bien que les étudiants participent en classe.

_____ 5. Pour devenir avocat, on va à l'École des Beaux-Arts.

_____ 6. Pour être admis à une Grande École, il faut passer un concours.

_____ 7. Pour suivre des cours à distance, on s'inscrit à un cours en ligne.

_____ 8. La calculatrice est inutile dans les cours de mathématiques.

## 4.3

*L'instruction.* Choose the best answer to complete each sentence.

1. On apprend le fonctionnement du corps humain en cours d' _____ .                a. casques

2. Quand on est faible dans une matière, il faut _____ .                b. collège

3. L' _____ à ce cours virtuel coûte très cher.                c. anatomie

4. M. Dupont travaille sur son _____ portable à tous moments.                d. immobilier

5. Au labo de langues, on met des _____ pour écouter des cassettes.                e. s'appliquer

6. Les étudiants de langue apprennent le _____ et la grammaire.                f. ordinateur

7. Après l'école élémentaire et avant le lycée, il y a le _____ .                g. abonnement

8. Il passe son temps à vendre des maisons. Il travaille dans l' _____ .                h. vocabulaire

## 4.4

*Les mots apparentés.* Find a noun having the same root as each preceding verb.

Example: lire/la lecture (read/reading)

1. remplacer _____

2. expliquer _____

3. dessiner _____

4. calculer _____

5. connaître _____

6. danser _____

7. enseigner _____

8. discuter _____

## 4.5

*Les fournitures scolaires.* Fill in the blank with the appropriate French word for the school supplies and materials needed in each case.

1. pour apporter les livres et les cahiers à l'école _____

2. pour tailler le crayon _____

3. pour mettre en valeur certains mots sur la page _____

4. pour prendre des notes _____

5. pour effacer une erreur sur le papier _____

6. pour traduire un mot _____

7. pour interpréter la langue de l'ordinateur _____

8. pour imprimer une page d'un site web _____

9. pour éviter qu'un virus attaque l'ordinateur _____

10. pour écouter le CD _____

## 4.6

*En classe.* Put these sentences in sequential order from A through E to reflect a class activity.

_____ 1. Les élèves vont à la récréation.

_____ 2. Les étudiants passent l'examen.

_____ 3. Le prof passe les copies de l'examen.

_____ 4. La classe commence.

_____ 5. Le prof ramasse les examens.

## 4.7

*À l'école.* Answer the following questions in French.

1. Quelle est ta matière favorite? _____

2. Où vas-tu à l'école? _____

3. Quelle est ta classe la plus difficile? _____

4. Sur quoi est-ce que le prof écrit souvent? _____

5. Qu'est-ce que tu as dans ton cartable? _____

6. Dans quoi est-ce que tu prends des notes? _____

7. Quand fais-tu tes devoirs? _____

8. Est-ce que tu as toujours de bonnes notes? _____

## 4.8

*Les études de Pierre.* Use the letters A through G to indicate the chronological order in which Pierre completed the various stages of his education.

_____ 1. Il va à la faculté de médecine.

_____ 2. Il termine le cycle élémentaire.

_____ 3. Il reçoit un diplôme universitaire.

_____ 4. Il choisit ses cours au lycée.

_____ 5. Il termine le cycle secondaire.

_____ 6. Il apprend à lire.

_____ 7. Il fait un stage comme médecin.

## 5.1

_J'achète un costume._ Use the letters A through J to put the following sentences in the correct order creating a conversation between a salesperson and a customer. Start with the salesperson greeting the gentleman, and end with the customer thanking the saleslady.

_____ 1. En effet! Il me faut un costume pour une soirée très chic.

_____ 2. Je suis sûre de pouvoir vous trouver un costume à votre goût. Nous n'avons que la meilleure qualité et la dernière mode.

_____ 3. Avec plaisir, monsieur. Veuillez me suivre! Quelle taille faites-vous?

_____ 4. Avez-vous une préférence de style et de couleur, monsieur?

_____ 5. Je vous fais confiance, mademoiselle, et je vous remercie d'avance!

_____ 6. Bonjour monsieur. Puis-je vous aider?

_____ 7. Je fais du quarante-quatre.

_____ 8. Bonjour, mademoiselle. Oui, pourriez-vous me montrer vos plus beaux costumes?

_____ 9. Alors, voilà les costumes dans votre taille. C'est pour une occasion spéciale?

_____ 10. Oui, je voudrais un costume noir en laine. Quelque chose de classique.

## 5.2

_Dans les magasins et services de vente._ Indicate True (_Vrai_) or False (_Faux_) for each sentence.

_____ 1. Acheter quelque chose au rabais, c'est acheter moins cher.

_____ 2. On porte une robe de chambre pour aller travailler.

_____ 3. À une vente aux enchères, c'est celui qui offre le plus d'argent qui reçoit l'objet.

_____ 4. On essaie des habits dans l'ascenseur.

_____ 5. Tout le monde arrive à l'heure de fermeture des magasins.

_____ 6. On achète des livres à la bibliothèque.

_____ 7. Le tapissier répare des divans et des fauteuils.

_____ 8. Avant d'offrir un cadeau, on l'emballe avec du papier-cadeau.

## 5.3

_Où aller pour trouver ce qu'on cherche?_ Where would you find each of the following items?

| | | | |
|---|---|---|---|
| _____ 1. | une lampe d'occasion | a. | à la quincaillerie |
| _____ 2. | un cadeau pour une future mariée | b. | à la papeterie |
| _____ 3. | un collier en or | c. | au marché |
| _____ 4. | un marteau | d. | à la boutique de mariage |
| _____ 5. | un beau sac en cuir | e. | à la bijouterie |
| _____ 6. | le médicament prescrit par le médecin | f. | au marché aux puces |
| _____ 7. | le journal | g. | à la maroquinerie |
| _____ 8. | des fruits frais | h. | à la pharmacie |

## 5.4

_Les petits magasins alimentaires._ Place each food on the appropriate line corresponding to the store where it can be found.

| la dinde | le jambon | la crevette | l'huile | l'huître |
|---|---|---|---|---|
| le pâté | l'agneau | le petit pain | le sel | le gâteau |

Boucherie: _____  _____

Charcuterie: _____  _____

Boulangerie-Pâtisserie: _____ _____

Poissonnerie: _____ _____

Épicerie: _____ _____

## 5.5

*La tenue vestimentaire.* Circle the correct meaning of each French word.

1. à carreaux     striped     polka dot     checkered
2. la soie        silk        velvet        sateen
3. large          long        tight         loose
4. court          short       rough         shrunk
5. la manche      waist       sleeve        hem
6. le tissu       clothes     look          cloth
7. l'écharpe      sock        scarf         coat
8. la pantoufle   slipper     sneaker       dress shoe

## 5.6

*Quelle est la solution à ces petits problèmes?* Choose the best word to complete each sentence.

tailleur     raccommoder     retoucher     repasser     laver

1. Ma chemise s'est déchirée. Je vais la _____.

2. Ce pantalon est froissé. Il faut le _____.

3. Tu as une grosse tache de jus sur ta blouse. Je vais la
   _____.

4. La fermeture-éclair de cette robe ne marche plus. Apporte-la chez le
   _____.

5. Je vais acheter ce costume, mais il faut _____ les
   manches qui sont trop longues.

## 5.7

*Les bijoux et les produits de beauté.* Circle the word that does not belong in each series.

1. l'alliance          la montre          l'anneau          la bague
2. le collier          le pendentif       le bracelet       la chaîne
3. le rubis            l'émeraude         la broche         le diamant
4. le crayon yeux      le rimmel          la poudre         le fard à paupières
5. le gel coiffant     la laque           la teinture       la pince

## 5.8

*Quelle est la question?* Choose the letter indicating the question for each of the following answers.

_____ 1. Non, cette couleur est trop criarde.

_____ 2. Au rayon librairie.

_____ 3. Oui, passez à la caisse, s'il vous plaît.

_____ 4. Non, ce n'est pas la bonne pointure.

_____ 5. Un costume élégant!

_____ 6. Non, une robe plutôt.

_____ 7. Trop tard. C'est fermé!

_____ 8. Non, il est trop cher.

a. Désirez-vous ces sandales jaunes?

b. Tu ne vas pas acheter ce foulard?

c. On va à la parfumerie?

d. Qu'est-ce que tu vas porter ce soir?

e. Vous cherchez une jupe?

f. Ce chemisier rouge me va bien?

g. Puis-je payer avec ma carte de crédit?

h. Où est-ce que je peux trouver un dictionnaire?

## 5.9

*La tenue d'occasion.* What garments should these people buy for the following activities and occasions?

_____ 1. pour faire de l'exercice     a. un sweat

_____ 2. pour une soirée très chic     b. un short

_____ 3. pour nager     c. un ensemble neuf

_____ 4. pour sortir sous la pluie     d. un pyjama

_____ 5. pour une réunion d'affaires     e. un maillot de bain

_____ 6. quand il fait très chaud     f. une robe longue

_____ 7. pour aller se coucher     g. un pull

_____ 8. s'il fait très froid     h. un imperméable

## 5.10

*Pour homme ou pour femme?* Indicate whether the garment is more likely to be worn by a man (M), a woman (W), or both (MW).

_____ 1. la jupe

_____ 2. l'imperméable

_____ 3. le tailleur

_____ 4. la chemise

_____ 5. le smoking

_____ 6. la chaussette

## 5.11

*La beauté.* Indicate whether these statements are True (*Vrai*) or False (*Faux*).

_____ 1. Le fond de teint est un produit de maquillage.

_____ 2. Si tu as la peau sèche, achète-toi une crème hydratante.

_____ 3. Le vernis se met sur les ongles.

_____ 4. Le rimmel se met sur les lèvres.

_____ 5. Une esthéticienne reçoit un pourboire.

_____ 6. La manicure sert du vin.

## 6.1

_Du plus petit au plus grand._ Rank the following from smallest to largest (from A to E).

_____ 1. gratte-ciel

_____ 2. maison à quatre étages

_____ 3. studio

_____ 4. duplex

_____ 5. toilettes

## 6.2

_Les pièces et les chambres du logement._ In which part of a home are you likely to do the following activities?

1. se mettre du rouge à lèvres: _____

2. préparer une omelette: _____

3. profiter du soleil sans quitter l'appartement: _____

4. bavarder avec ses amis en écoutant des CD: _____

5. se coucher et dormir: _____

## 6.3

_À la maison._ Choose the word that best completes each sentence.

fenêtre   salon   grenier   immeuble   toit   clé

1. Je vis dans un nouvel _____ dans la rue de la Pierre.

2. Anne a mis ses vieux meubles au _____.

3. J'aime bien le tableau que tu as dans ton _____.

4. Ouvre donc la _____ de ta chambre!

5. Installe l'antenne de télévision sur le _____.

6. C'est la _____ de l'entrée principale.

## 6.4

*À quoi ça sert?* Choose the activity that you can perform with each appliance.

_____ 1. le radiateur        a. aérer

_____ 2. l'aspirateur        b. nettoyer

_____ 3. le congélateur        c. chauffer l'air

_____ 4. la cuisinière        d. faire une omelette

_____ 5. le ventilateur        e. congeler de la nourriture

## 6.5

*La routine quotidienne.* Translate the following sentences into French.

1. I take out the garbage every day. _____

2. Anne turns on the light on the terrace. _____

3. We have a new refrigerator. _____

4. The towel is dirty. _____

5. I have to tidy up my bedroom. _____

6. We don't often wash the windows in the living room.

   _____

7. Do you cook on weekends? _____

8. I need a broom and a dustpan. _____

## 6.6

*Chez nous.* Indicate True (*Vrai*) or False (*Faux*) for each sentence.

_____ 1. Le drap couvre la table.

_____ 2. La glace est sur le parquet.

_____ 3. Les livres sont sur l'étagère.

_____ 4. Les invités sont assis sur le fer à repasser.

_____ 5. On lave les assiettes dans le lavabo.

_____ 6. On fait la lessive dans la machine à laver.

_____ 7. La femme de ménage cire la vaisselle.

_____ 8. On arrose le tapis.

## 6.7

*Dans la cuisine.* Circle the appropriate English translation for each of the following household items.

| | | | |
|---|---|---|---|
| 1. l'éponge | detergent | sponge | brush |
| 2. la cuillère | pot | oven | spoon |
| 3. les couverts | fork | tablecloth | cutlery |
| 4. les serviettes | pans | napkins | matches |
| 5. la pelle | dustpan | brush | broom |
| 6. le plateau | dish | tray | teapot |

## 6.8

*Comment vis-tu?* Répondez aux questions en français.

1. Tu vis dans un appartement ou dans une maison?

   _____

2. Tu paies un loyer ou une hypothèque? _____

3. Tu as un micro-ondes chez toi? _____

4. Est-ce qu'il y a un balcon dans ta chambre à coucher?

   _____

5. Tu laves la vaisselle dans l'évier ou dans le lave-vaisselle?

_____

6. Tu regardes la télé dans ton salon ou dans ta chambre à coucher?

_____

## 7.1

*Les occupations.* Indicate True (*Vrai*) or False (*Faux*) for each sentence.

_____ 1. Les coiffeurs s'occupent de vos cheveux.

_____ 2. Les bibliothécaires travaillent toujours dans des librairies.

_____ 3. Le facteur distribue le courrier.

_____ 4. L'instituteur enseigne la philosophie.

_____ 5. Le boulanger vend du pain.

_____ 6. La couturière fait des retouches et des habits sur mesure.

_____ 7. Le couvreur vend des livres.

_____ 8. Le cordonnier répare les chaussures.

_____ 9. Le jardinier utilise une lime, des vis et des clous.

_____ 10. Le maçon a besoin d'une bétonnière.

## 7.2

*Où, qui et quoi?* Choose the matching definition for each word.

_____ 1. la caisse

_____ 2. le jardinier

_____ 3. le classeur

_____ 4. l'en-tête

_____ 5. l'atelier

a. Là où travaille l'artisan.

b. Le nom de la société sur une lettre.

c. Là où on paie.

d. L'homme qui s'occupe des plantes et de l'herbe.

e. Là où on met les chemises et les documents.

## 7.3

*Au travail.* Write the letter corresponding to the appropriate answer to each of the following questions.

_____ 1. L'imprimante ne marche pas?     a. Oui, copie-le sur une disquette!

_____ 2. Je peux rédiger ce document chez moi?     b. Mais non, au stylo bien sûr!

_____ 3. Où est cette adresse?     c. Mets la nouvelle cartouche.

_____ 4. Tu vas signer au crayon?     d. Oui, voilà l'agrafeuse!

_____ 5. Ces deux fiches vont ensemble?     e. Regarde donc dans le fichier.

## 7.4

*Les conditions de travail.* Circle the correct English translation for each French word.

| | | | |
|---|---|---|---|
| 1. l'augmentation | strike | layoff | raise |
| 2. le traitement | advance | salary | credit |
| 3. les congés maladie | sick leave | resignation | pension |
| 4. l'hypothèque | layoff | union | mortgage |
| 5. le boulot | job | advance | minimum wage |
| 6. la grève | payroll | strike | unemployment |
| 7. l'offre d'emploi | vacancy | vacation | wages |
| 8. la retraite | promotion | retirement | advance |
| 9. le syndicat | union | strike | severance |
| 10. faire le pont | demonstrate | get a bonus | take a long weekend |

## 7.5

*Les économies et les investissements.* Complete each sentence with the appropriate word from the list.

| | | | |
|---|---|---|---|
| intérêts | actions | versement | en hausse |
| dettes | économiser | épargne | prêt |

1. Je voudrais _____ de l'argent pour acheter une maison.

2. Je vais ouvrir un compte d' _____ au Crédit Mutuel aujourd'hui.

3. Je vais faire mon premier _____ dans ce compte immédiatement.

4. Je vais gagner des _____ sur mon compte d'épargne.

5. J'espère un jour obtenir un _____ pour acheter la maison de mes rêves.

6. J'ai acheté des _____ dans une société de communication.

7. Le coût de la vie est _____ à cause de l'inflation.

8. Je ne dois rien à personne. Je n'ai pas de _____.

## 7.6

*Les services bancaires.* Fill in the blank with the appropriate word from the following choices.

| | | | |
|---|---|---|---|
| prêt | relevé | échanger | coffre-fort |
| retirer | fonds | branche | accumuler |

1. Au taux actuel, mes investissements vont _____ des intérêts importants.

2. Tu as de l'argent dans ton compte en banque? Vérifie ton _____.

3. Si tu pars en France, n'oublie pas d' _____ des dollars en euros.

4. Cette _____ de la banque reste ouverte le samedi.

5. Il me faut un _____ de la banque pour acheter une nouvelle voiture.

6. Je garde tous mes bijoux à la banque, dans un _____.

7. Je suis au guichet en train de _____ $250 de mon compte bancaire.

8. Mon Dieu! Je n'ai plus de _____ dans mon compte en banque.

## 7.7

*Je cherche un emploi.* Starting with the letter A, arrange these sentences in logical order to create a telephone conversation between a young man and a prospective employer.

_____ 1. Chef comptable.

_____ 2. Quel emploi cherchez-vous?

_____ 3. Oui, bien sûr. Faut-il prendre rendez-vous?

_____ 4. Non, pas tout de suite. D'abord, vous allez remplir une fiche.

_____ 5. Bonjour, monsieur? Je téléphone à propos d'un emploi.

_____ 6. Il faut passer à notre bureau du personnel.

_____ 7. Et vous fournir un CV.

_____ 8. C'est ça. Ensuite on vous donnera rendez-vous pour un entretien.

## 7.8

*Fluctuations économiques.* Choose the word or expression that best completes the meaning of each of the following sentences.

réserve        faillite        salaire        coût de la vie   baissé

1. Nous ne pouvons pas acheter de nouvel équipement parce qu'il n'y a pas d'argent en _____.

2. Le prix de l'essence a _____ de 3 à 2 dollars. Super!

3. Augmenter le prix de la marchandise nous permet d'augmenter le
   _____ des employés.

4. Quand le _____ augmente, il nous faut une
   augmentation de salaire.

5. Nous allons tout perdre. C'est la _____.

## 8.1

*Qui est-ce?* Choose the letter for the corresponding definition.

_____ 1. Il joue du piano dans un       a. l'animateur
        orchestre.

_____ 2. Il écrit des romans.           b. l'informaticien

_____ 3. Il peint des paysages et       c. le romancier
        des natures mortes.

_____ 4. Il fait des statues de         d. l'auditeur
        personnages célèbres.

_____ 5. Il aide les gens avec leurs    e. le peintre
        problèmes d'ordinateur.

_____ 6. Il reçoit plusieurs bulletins  f. le musicien
        électroniques.

_____ 7. Il présente des invités à la   g. l'usager
        télé.

_____ 8. Il écoute la radio.            h. le sculpteur

## 8.2

*Les loisirs.* Indicate True (*Vrai*) or False (*Faux*) for each sentence.

_____ 1. Tintin est un personnage de bande dessinée.

_____ 2. On va dans les cybercafés pour admirer des œuvres d'art.

_____ 3. TV5 est une chaîne diffusée dans le monde francophone.

_____ 4. Yahoo est un moteur de recherche.

_____ 5. La disquette a plus de mémoire que le CD-ROM.

_____ 6. L'équipe brésilienne se qualifie souvent pour la Coupe du Monde de foot.

_____ 7. Les programmes anti-virus protègent les gens contre les maladies.

_____ 8. Le hockey sur glace se joue uniquement au Canada.

## 8.3

*Comment passer son temps libre?* Circle the word that does not belong in each series.

1. a. la distraction   b. le divertissement   c. la descente   d. les loisirs

2. a. le bowling   b. le vol libre   c. le golf   d. la pétanque

3. a. le cyclo-tourisme   b. la randonnée   c. la promenade   d. la marche

4. a. le volley-ball   b. le basket-ball   c. le water-polo   d. le football

5. a. le concert   b. le récital   c. la symphonie   d. les actualités

6. a. la souris   b. le droit d'accès   c. la touche   d. la vedette

7. a. les lettres   b. la piste   c. la bulle   d. l'article

8. a. le réveillon   b. le réchaud   c. le feu de camp   d. le plein air

9. a. le manège   b. l'œnologie   c. le cirque   d. le carrousel

10. a. se détendre   b. se reposer   c. se relaxer   d. se dépenser

## 8.4

*Nommez la fête!* Name the holiday!

1. Le jour où le Père Noël apporte des cadeaux aux enfants.

   _____

2. Le premier jour de la nouvelle année. _____

3. Le jour où tout le monde fait des blagues. _____

4. Le jour où on a le réveillon. _____

5. La fête du 14 juillet. _____

6. La fête des amoureux. _____

7. La fête du jour où on s'est marié. _____

8. Le(s) jour(s) où on se déguise et il y a des bals masqués.

_____

## 8.5

*Où aller?* Identify the place where you are likely to do the following activities.

1. danser le samedi soir: _____

2. regarder un film qui vient de sortir: _____

3. voir une collection d'art: _____

4. faire du patin à glace: _____

5. rencontrer des auteurs et entendre des discussions littéraires:

_____

## 8.6

*Au cinéma.* Match the answers on the left with the corresponding question on the right.

_____ 1. Parce que l'actrice a bien joué.

a. Tu ne veux pas regarder ce film?

_____ 2. Oui, c'est un film étranger.

b. Pourquoi tu pleures?

_____ 3. Ah non. C'est un navet!

c. Pourquoi est-ce que tu applaudis?

_____ 4. Non, c'est trop compliqué.

d. Tu trembles?

_____ 5. Ce film est si drôle!

e. Ce film est sous-titré?

_____ 6. Le guichet de vente est fermé.

f. Tu ne comprends pas l'intrigue?

_____ 7. La fin du film est vraiment triste.

g. Pourquoi tu n'achètes pas les billets?

_____ 8. Oui, j'ai peur pour l'héroïne!

h. Pourquoi est-ce que tu ris si fort?

## 8.7

*Au musée.* Starting with the letter A, arrange these sentences in logical order to create a dialogue between a student and a ticket agent at a museum.

_____ 1. Bonjour, madame. Deux entrées étudiantes, c'est combien?

_____ 2. Ça fait cinq euros de plus par personne.

_____ 3. Quelle chance! C'est combien pour une visite guidée?

_____ 4. C'est un prix spécial aujourd'hui?

_____ 5. Oui aujourd'hui, c'est 15% de rabais sur le prix normal.

_____ 6. Ne manquez pas de visiter la boutique au deuxième étage.

_____ 7. Alors, nous prenons les entrées et les visites guidées.

_____ 8. C'est douze euros au prix étudiant.

_____ 9. Bonne journée, mesdemoiselles.

_____ 10. Certainement, madame. Il nous faut des reproductions pour offrir comme cadeaux à nos parents.

## 8.8

*Les passe-temps.* Translate the following sentences.

1. I love going to the beach and swimming in the ocean.

   _____

2. Camping is fun. _____

3. Do you play checkers? _____

4. He collects old cars. _____

5. I like to chat with my friends on the Internet. _____

   _____

6. I read science fiction novels. _____

7. Shucks! I deleted an e-mail. _____

8. I jog in the park near my house. _____

9. My favorite team does not win all the time. _____

10. Crossword puzzles are sometimes difficult. _____

## 8.9

*Journaux, magazines et télévision.* Indicate whether these statements are True (*Vrai*) or False (*Faux*).

_____ 1. Tu peux lire ton avenir dans la section de la gastronomie.

_____ 2. L'horoscope te donne la liste des programmes de télévision.

_____ 3. Les nouvelles les plus récentes paraissent en première page dans le journal.

_____ 4. Le bulletin météorologique annonce le temps qu'il va faire.

_____ 5. Tu peux changer les chaînes de télévision avec l'auto-commande.

_____ 6. Si tu veux acheter une voiture, consulte la section immobilière.

_____ 7. On entend généralement des annonces publicitaires à la radio.

_____ 8. Beaucoup de revues comprennent des mots croisés.

## 8.10

*Le sport.* Circle the word that is related to each of the following activities.

1. le baseball:    le gant        le filet        la raquette

2. la natation:    la cour        la piscine      le terrain

3. l'escrime:      la batte       le but          l'épée

4. l'athlétisme:   la piste       la balle        la plongée

5. le football:    le patin       la piste        le gardien de but

6. le cyclisme:    le vélo        la moto         les baskets

## 8.11

*Au restaurant.* Answer the questions in French.

1. Quel est ton restaurant favori? _____

2. Est-ce que les portions sont généreuses? _____

3. Il est cher ou bon marché, ce restaurant? _____

4. Qu'est-ce que tu donnes comme pourboire à ton serveur?
   _____

5. Quel est le plat du jour? _____

6. Quelle est la spécialité de la maison? _____

## 9.1

*Les déplacements.* Rank each type of transportation, using numbers 1 through 5, starting with the fastest.

_____ 1. bac

_____ 2. bicyclette

_____ 3. avion

_____ 4. train (TGV)

_____ 5. voiture

## 9.2

*Dans la voiture.* Identify the part to be used to perform the following actions while driving a car.

_____ 1. ralentir                          a. l'accélérateur

_____ 2. démarrer                          b. l'huile

_____ 3. indiquer qu'on tourne à           c. le rétroviseur
        gauche

_____ 4. accélérer                          d. la clef de contact

_____ 5. s'attacher                         e. l'essuie-glace

| | | | |
|---|---|---|---|
| _____ | 6. voir ce qui vient derrière | f. | les freins |
| _____ | 7. nettoyer le pare-brise s'il pleut | g. | le clignoteur |
| _____ | 8. lubrifier le moteur | h. | la ceinture de sécurité |

## 9.3

*Savez-vous conduire?* Indicate whether each statement is True (*Vrai*) or False (*Faux*).

_____ 1. Il faut un permis de conduire pour rouler en vélo.

_____ 2. Quand il y a beaucoup de circulation, il faut faire des queues de poisson pour aller plus vite.

_____ 3. Il y a généralement des péages sur l'autoroute.

_____ 4. On peut écraser les piétons dans les passages à piétons.

_____ 5. On conduit toujours sur le trottoir.

_____ 6. Dans une rue à sens unique, la circulation ne va que dans une seule direction.

_____ 7. Les bouchons causent des retards.

_____ 8. Il faut s'arrêter aux feux verts.

## 9.4

*Vive les vacances!* Complete each sentence with an appropriate word from the list.

| | | | |
|---|---|---|---|
| périmé | agence | syndicat | forfait |
| hors-taxe | change | brochures | vacances |

1. Je voudrais des _____ sur les croisières en Méditerrannée.

2. Je préfère les voyages à _____ où tout est compris.

3. Je vais écrire au _____ d'initiative de Marseille pour me renseigner.

4. Je peux aussi aller dans une _____ de voyages pour obtenir des renseignements.

5. Il vaut mieux que je vérifie que mon passeport n'est pas _____.

6. Je prendrai des euros au bureau du _____ de l'aéroport.

7. Au retour, je veux acheter du parfum dans une boutique _____.

8. Quelles belles _____ je vais passer!

## 9.5

*Les voyages.* Circle the correct meaning(s) for each French word.

| | | | |
|---|---|---|---|
| 1. la surréservation | overbooking | upgrade | surcharge |
| 2. l'atterrissage | takeoff | landing | emergency |
| 3. l'escale | departure | arrival | stopover |
| 4. les écouteurs | loudspeakers | headset | passengers |
| 5. l'abonnement | registration | rate | commuter pass |
| 6. le quai | platform | landing strip | dock |
| 7. la gare | bus station | train station | boarding gate |
| 8. la bouée | life jacket | safety belt | life buoy |
| 9. la marée | tide | marine | sea |
| 10. le paquebot | ocean liner | safety boat | sailboat |

## 9.6

*Que vous faut-il?* What do you need in the following situations while traveling by boat or by train? Indicate the letter of the most appropriate answer.

_____ 1. Le train va partir bientôt.    a. une couchette

_____ 2. Je veux dormir pendant la nuit.    b. une place en TGV

_____ 3. Je voudrais raccourcir la durée de mon trajet.

c. une traversée en ferry

_____ 4. Le bateau risque de faire naufrage.

d. le quai et la voie corrects

_____ 5. Je voudrais visiter le port.

e. le gilet de sauvetage

## 9.7

_À l'hôtel._ Choose the appropriate answer for each question asked by a hotel guest.

_____ 1. Où est la réception?

a. Appelez le service de blanchisserie.

_____ 2. Que faire de mon linge sale?

b. Je vois que vous connaissez l'hôtel.

_____ 3. Pourquoi cet hôtel est-il si cher?

c. C'est un hôtel à trois étoiles.

_____ 4. Tu as réglé la note de la chambre?

d. Dans le hall, à droite.

_____ 5. La suite 2000 est-elle disponible?

e. Oui, je l'ai fait ce matin.

_____ 6. Il me faut de l'aide avec mes bagages.

f. Oui, mais elle n'a pas de vue sur la mer.

_____ 7. Il n'y a pas d'ascenseur?

g. Je vous appelle un chasseur.

_____ 8. Est-ce qu'il vous reste une chambre?

h. Si, au bout du couloir à gauche.

## 10.1

_Nation et gouvernement._ Indicate True (_Vrai_) or False (_Faux_) for each statement.

_____ 1. Le gouvernement américain est basé sur le principe de la séparation des pouvoirs.

_____ 2. La France a une dictature.

_____ 3. La Marseillaise est l'hymne national du Canada.

_____ 4. En France, un président doit être élu au suffrage universel.

_____ 5. Aux États-Unis, on a le droit de voter à partir de vingt et un ans.

_____ 6. Le parti communiste est un parti de gauche.

_____ 7. Le vice-président exerce les fonctions que lui confie le président.

_____ 8. Aucun pays n'accepte qu'un citoyen ait une double nationalité.

_____ 9. Un immigrant clandestin court le risque d'être déporté.

_____ 10. Un immigrant doit obtenir un permis de travail du pays d'asile.

## 10.2

_Comment fonctionne un gouvernement?_ Complete each statement with the appropriate word from the list.

secrétaire          cinq          président     cabinet        roi

1. Le _____ des États-Unis est le chef de la branche exécutive.

2. Le président choisit les membres de son _____.

3. Aux États-Unis le/la _____ d'État est nommé(e) par le président.

4. Il y a un _____ en Espagne.

5. Les Français élisent un nouveau président tous les _____ ans.

## 10.3

_Que me faut-il?_ What do you need in these situations? Choose the appropriate letter.

_____ 1. Il me faut un visa pour la Chine.  a. un numéro de sécurité sociale

_____ 2. Je dois payer mes impôts.      b. un certificat de naissance

_____ 3. Il me faut une preuve          c. un permis de travail
        de ma nationalité.

_____ 4. Je veux travailler dans un      d. un consulat
        pays étranger.

_____ 5. J'ai perdu mon passeport.

## 10.4

*Les revendications.* Complete each sentence with an appropriate word from the list.

médiateurs          salariés          syndicat          compromis          boycott

1. Le _____ manifeste le mécontentement d'un groupe de personnes.

2. Il faut arriver à un _____ pour éviter une grève.

3. Après la grève, les _____ reprennent le travail.

4. Les _____ ont mené les négociations et ont trouvé une solution au conflit.

5. Les ouvriers de cette société versent une cotisation à leur _____.

## 10.5

*Un délit!* Number the events in the most logical chronological order, from 1 to 10, and reconstitute the story of a crime.

_____ 1. Le détective l'emmène au commissariat.

_____ 2. Finalement il reçoit une peine de prison de trois à cinq ans.

_____ 3. Il rôde dans le quartier.

_____ 4. Son avocat vient le voir en prison.

_____ 5. Il cambriole une maison.

_____ 6. Le procureur demande la réclusion pour ce récidiviste.

_____ 7. Il est inculpé. On ouvre un casier judiciaire.

_____ 8. Il y a un procès.

_____ 9. Un voisin téléphone à la police.

_____ 10. Il est pris en flagrant délit.

## 10.6

_La paix et les menaces à la paix._ Choose the appropriate word from the list to complete each sentence.

| | | | | |
|---|---|---|---|---|
| paix | guerre | puissance | sanctions | accord |
| otages | métier | militaire | piégée | victimes |

1. Les États-Unis sont une grande _____ mondiale.

2. Une réunion au sommet est prévue pour discuter de _____ contre un pays qui défie les conventions internationales.

3. Un traité de _____ a été signé après un armistice entre les deux nations.

4. Plusieurs pays ont conclu un _____ pour enrayer la prolifération des armes nucléaires.

5. Les crimes de _____ sont impardonnables.

6. L'armée américaine est une armée de _____.

7. D'innocentes personnes sont les _____ d'attentats terroristes.

8. Une opération de sauvetage a permis de retrouver des _____.

9. Une voiture _____ a causé l'effondrement d'un immeuble administratif.

10. Le service _____ est obligatoire en Israël.

## 10.7

*La guerre.* Translate the following sentences into French.

1. Diplomacy is the best means to preserve peace. _____

2. The summit meeting takes place in New York. _____

3. They are going to sign a peace treaty soon. _____

4. In each war there are conscientious objectors. _____

5. Defeat is always humiliating. _____

6. Hostilities continue. _____

7. We are going to win the war. _____

8. They declared a state of emergency. _____

9. The aircraft carrier is in the gulf. _____

10. They just caught a spy. _____

## 11.1

*La terre.* Choose the appropriate word from the list to complete each sentence.

| grottes | étoiles | galaxies | l'embouchure | lune |
|---------|---------|----------|--------------|------|
| montagnes | ruisseaux | étangs | occidentale | nord |

1. La nuit, les _____ brillent dans le ciel.

2. Ce soir on ne voit qu'un croissant de _____ .

3. Il y a beaucoup de _____ dans l'univers.

4. On trouve des _____ préhistoriques en France.

5. Les _____ les plus hautes d'Europe sont les Alpes.

6. Les _____ coulent dans les rivières.

7. La ville de Bordeaux se trouve à _____ de la Garonne.

8. Monet a peint beaucoup de tableaux avec des _____ .

9. Une boussole indique toujours le _____ .

10. La France est située en Europe _____ .

## 11.2

*Les conditions météorologiques.* Identify and circle the word that does not belong in each series.

| | | | |
|---|---|---|---|
| 1. la glace | la foudre | le gel | l'iceberg |
| 2. l'inondation | la pluie | le vent | le nuage |
| 3. doux | beau | ensoleillé | orageux |
| 4. le séisme | le tonnerre | le cyclone | l'ouragan |
| 5. le degré | la chaleur | la fraîcheur | la latitude |

## 11.3

*L'environnement.* Indicate True (*Vrai*) or False (*Faux*) for each sentence.

_____ 1. Le recyclage aide à préserver les ressources naturelles.

_____ 2. Il n'y a plus d'espèces en danger sur terre.

_____ 3. L'écologiste défend l'environnement.

_____ 4. Les trous dans la couche d'ozone causent des cancers de la peau.

_____ 5. Le déboisement cause des dégâts sur les récifs de corail.

_____ 6. La décharge de produits chimiques dans la nature cause la contamination de l'eau potable.

_____ 7. Les accidents nucléaires sont rarement nocifs.

_____ 8. Le braconnage est favorable aux espèces en danger.

_____ 9. La marée noire est un océan.

_____ 10. Les déchets industriels menacent la faune et la flore.

## 11.4

*Quel est le contraire?* Determine which of the following pairs are opposites.

_____ 1. l'été            a. au soleil

_____ 2. la chaleur     b. sauvage

_____ 3. tropical          c. l'hiver

_____ 4. à l'ombre      d. polaire

_____ 5. domestique    e. la fraîcheur

## 11.5

_Quel est le synonyme?_ Determine which of the following pairs are synonyms.

_____ 1. le bois         a. cueillir les raisins

_____ 2. le pâturage    b. vaporiser

_____ 3. récolter       c. le pré

_____ 4. vendanger    d. le cultivateur

_____ 5. le fermier     e. moissonner

_____ 6. asperger     f. la forêt

## 11.6

_Fruits et légumes._ Indicate _V_ for a vegetable or _F_ for a fruit.

_____ 1. la groseille

_____ 2. la betterave

_____ 3. la framboise

_____ 4. la fraise

_____ 5. le pamplemousse

_____ 6. le chou

_____ 7. l'oignon

_____ 8. le poireau

_____ 9. l'ananas

_____ 10. le haricot

## 11.7

*Le monde de la nature.* Circle the word that does not belong.

1. le lilas        le muguet       l'œillet        le chêne

2. le palmier      le tilleul      la tulipe       le pin

3. le dindon       le taureau      le bœuf         le veau

4. le lapin        le poussin      la poule        le coq

5. le vautour      l'autruche      l'aigle         le condor

6. la baleine      le dauphin      le requin       la moufette

## 11.8

*Mon jardin.* Put these sentences in logical order using letters A through F.

_____ 1. Les plantes de tomates sont malades.

_____ 2. J'utilise un insecticide.

_____ 3. J'achète les graines.

_____ 4. Les tomates mûrissent.

_____ 5. J'arrose les graines tous les jours.

_____ 6. Je plante les graines.

## 11.9

*Les fleurs et les arbres.* Choose the appropriate English word that identifies each of the trees and flowers in a garden.

_____ 1. le tournesol          a. olive tree

_____ 2. le pommier            b. mahogany

_____ 3. l'œillet              c. sunflower

_____ 4. le palmier            d. lily

_____ 5. l'olivier             e. hydrangea

_____ 6. l'hortensia           f. palm tree

_____ 7. l'acajou              g. elm

_____ 8. le lys　　　h. carnation

_____ 9. l'orme　　　i. apple tree

_____ 10. le coquelicot　　j. poppy

## 11.10

_Notre planète._ Translate the following phrases into French.

1. The coastal area is a desolate region. _____

2. Dr. Ray studies volcanoes. _____

3. We need more rainforest. _____

4. This region is mountainous. _____

5. She fell down the slope. _____

6. The river floods the valley every spring. _____

7. The water in the pond is polluted. _____

8. We swim upstream. _____

9. The waves are high. _____

10. Let's take a picture of the waterfall. _____

## 12.1

_Quel est le contraire?_ Determine which words are opposites.

_____ 1. long　　　a. minuscule

_____ 2. lâche　　　b. léger

_____ 3. haut　　　c. plus

_____ 4. trop　　　d. serré

_____ 5. gigantesque　　e. beaucoup

_____ 6. lourd　　　f. bas

_____ 7. peu　　　g. court

_____ 8. moins　　　h. pas assez

## 12.2

*Comment mesurez-vous?* Choose the word from the list that best completes the sentence.

pincée        bouchée      bouteille     douzaine

autant        grammes      soixantaine   tranches

1. Ils ont bu toute une _____ de vin.

2. Il me faut 200 _____ de farine pour faire des crêpes.

3. Achète-moi une _____ d'œufs. Je vais faire des gâteaux.

4. Je pense que ce vieux monsieur a la _____.

5. Prends au moins une _____ de ce pain pour goûter.

6. Ne mets pas plus d'une _____ de sel dans cette salade.

7. Quelques _____ de jambon, s'il vous plaît!

8. Je n'ai jamais vu _____ de chocolat de ma vie!

## 12.3

*Savez-vous compter?* Indicate True (*Vrai*) or False (*Faux*) for each sentence.

_____ 1. Deux moins deux est une addition.

_____ 2. Trois fois trois est une multiplication.

_____ 3. La somme de tous les angles d'un triangle est égale à 180 degrés.

_____ 4. Le nombre neuf est pair.

_____ 5. Une matinée est la première fois qu'on voit un film.

_____ 6. Un siècle fait cent années.

## 12.4

*Les mesures.* Write the letter of the appropriate French translation for each of the following words.

_____ 1. height a. la longueur b. le mètre c. la hauteur

_____ 2. depth a. la dimension b. la profondeur c. la moyenne

_____ 3. scale a. la largeur b. la balance c. la taille

_____ 4. weight a. le poids b. la livre c. la tonne

_____ 5. spoonful a. la bouteille b. la cuillerée c. le verre

## 12.5

*Quelle est la question?* Choose the question that corresponds to each of the following answers.

_____ 1. Trente pour cent de mon salaire.

a. Quelle est la grandeur de la Tour Eiffel?

_____ 2. Non merci! Un seul suffit.

b. Tu bois un second verre de vin?

_____ 3. Elle fait plus de trois cents mètres.

c. Une douzaine d'œufs, madame?

_____ 4. Oui, elle est chère, n'est-ce pas?

d. Tu as besoin de beaucoup d'essence?

_____ 5. Non, juste assez pour rentrer à la maison.

e. Combien est-ce que tu paies en taxe?

_____ 6. Non, deux, s'il vous plaît.

f. Cette auto vaut trente mille euros?

## 12.6

*Les nombres cardinaux.* Write the letter that matches the number spelled in French.

_____ 1. trente-cinq a. 15

_____ 2. soixante-sept b. 16

_____ 3. seize                                c. 1,000,000,000

_____ 4. un milliard                          d. 1,000,000

_____ 5. cent vingt-cinq                      e. 80

_____ 6. cinq cent quarante                   f. 70

_____ 7. quinze                               g. 67

_____ 8. soixante-dix                         h. 35

_____ 9. un million                           i. 125

_____ 10. quatre-vingts                       j. 540

## 12.7

_Les nombres ordinaux._ Translate the following sentences into French.

1. It's on the first floor. _____

2. Today is the fourth of July. _____

3. The tenth chapter is fun. _____

4. The fifth game was the best. _____

5. I like the horse in the ninth race. _____

6. This is not the twentieth century any more. _____

7. This is the second week of the month. _____

8. November is the eleventh month of the year. _____

# Answer Key

## 1.1

| 1. c | 2. e | 3. d | 4. a | 5. b |

## 1.2

| 1. 2 | 2. 6 | 3. 8 | 4. 4 | 5. 3 |
| 6. 1 | 7. 5 | 8. 7 | | |

## 1.3

| 1. V | 2. F | 3. F | 4. V | 5. F |
| 6. V | 7. V | 8. V | 9. V | 10. F |

## 1.4

| 1. h | 2. g | 3. c | 4. f | 5. b |
| 6. d | 7. a | 8. e | | |

## 1.5

Check numbers 3 and 5

## 1.6

| 1. b | 2. b | 3. d | 4. b | 5. a |
| 6. b | 7. c | 8. b | 9. a | 10. c |

## 1.7

| 1. c | 2. e | 3. a | 4. b | 5. d |

## 1.8

| 1. tien | 2. toi | 3. me | 4. tiens | 5. Lequel |

## 2.1

| 1. c | 2. f | 3. h | 4. g | 5. i |
| 6. j | 7. a | 8. d | 9. b | 10. e |

## 2.2

| 1. c | 2. d | 3. b | 4. a | 5. c |
|------|------|------|------|------|

## 2.3

1. créative/artistique  2. antipathique 3. impatient   4. courageuse
5. patient/persévérant

## 2.4

| 1. i | 2. d | 3. h | 4. f | 5. c |
|------|------|------|------|------|
| 6. j | 7. e | 8. a | 9. g | 10. b |

## 2.5

| 1. F | 2. V | 3. V | 4. V | 5. F |
|------|------|------|------|------|

## 2.6

| 1. a | 2. a | 3. c | 4. b | 5. c |
|------|------|------|------|------|

## 2.7

| 1. g | 2. h | 3. f | 4. c | 5. d |
|------|------|------|------|------|
| 6. a | 7. e | 8. b | | |

## 3.1

| 1. d | 2. e | 3. b | 4. a | 5. c |
|------|------|------|------|------|

## 3.2

| 1. cils | 2. paupières | 3. cou | 4. chauve | 5. joue |
|---------|--------------|--------|-----------|---------|
| 6. ventre | 7. coudes | 8. cheville | 9. oignon | 10. poignet |

## 3.3

| 1. c | 2. d | 3. a | 4. e | 5. b |
|------|------|------|------|------|

## 3.4

| | | | | |
|---|---|---|---|---|
| 1. le goût | 2. le goût | 3. l'odorat | 4. le toucher | 5. l'ouïe |
| 6. la vue | 7. le goût | 8. l'odorat | 9. l'ouïe | 10. la vue |

## 3.5

1. Je me rince la gorge.
2. Je me brosse les dents avec ma nouvelle brosse à dents.
3. Je me rase avec mon rasoir électrique.
4. Je prends une douche.
5. Mon savon sent bon.
6. J'ai besoin d'une serviette propre.
7. Oh, non! Je n'ai pas de déodorant.
8. Où sont les ciseaux?
9. Et maintenant je vais me tailler la moustache.
10. Et je vais me limer les ongles.

## 3.6

| | | | | |
|---|---|---|---|---|
| 1. D | 2. C | 3. G | 4. A | 5. F |
| 6. B | 7. E | | | |

## 3.7

| | | | | |
|---|---|---|---|---|
| 1. get better | 2. drowsiness | 3. blood | 4. wound | 5. pain |
| 6. queasiness | 7. swollen | 8. weak | 9. flu | 10. cough |

## 3.8

| | | | | |
|---|---|---|---|---|
| 1. sourde-muette | 2. symptômes de retrait | 3. myope | 4. diagnostic | 5. syrop |
| 6. oreillons | 7. repos | 8. secours | 9. paraplégique | |
| 10. caries | | | | |

## 3.9

1. le/la cardiologue
2. le docteur/l'infirmier/ l'infirmière
3. le/la chirurgien(ne) dentaire
4. la sage-femme
5. le/la diététicien(ne)
6. l'ambulancier
7. le/la chirurgien(ne)
8. le/la généraliste
9. le/la technicien(ne) radiologique
10. le chercheur

## 3.10

1. nouveau-né
2. enfant en bas âge
3. âge de raison
4. adolescent
5. majeur
6. adulte
7. troisième âge
8. décédé
9. funérailles
10. enterrement/incinération

## 4.1

1. d
2. a
3. e
4. b
5. a, d
6. b
7. c
8. a

## 4.2

1. V
2. F
3. V
4. V
5. F
6. V
7. V
8. F

## 4.3

1. c
2. e
3. g
4. f
5. a
6. h
7. b
8. d

## 4.4

1. le/la remplaçant(e)
2. l'explication
3. le dessin
4. le calcul/la calculatrice
5. la connaissance
6. la danse
7. l'enseignement
8. la discussion

**4.5**

1. un cartable
2. un taille-crayon
3. un surligneur
4. un stylo/un crayon /un ordinateur
5. une gomme/un correcteur blanc
6. un dictionnaire
7. un logiciel
8. une imprimante
9. un programme anti-virus
10. un lecteur de CD/un CD-ROM

**4.6**

| 1. E | 2. C | 3. B | 4. A | 5. D |

**4.7**

Answers will vary.

**4.8**

| 1. F | 2. B | 3. E | 4. C | 5. D |
| 6. A | 7. G | | | |

**5.1**

| 1. F | 2. I | 3. C | 4. G | 5. J |
| 6. A | 7. D | 8. B | 9. E | 10. H |

**5.2**

| 1. V | 2. F | 3. V | 4. F | 5. F |
| 6. F | 7. V | 8. V | | |

**5.3**

| 1. f | 2. d | 3. e | 4. a | 5. g |
| 6. h | 7. b | 8. c | | |

## 5.4

| | | |
|---|---|---|
| Boucherie: | la dinde | l'agneau |
| Charcuterie: | le jambon | le pâté |
| Boulangerie-Pâtisserie: | le petit pain | le gâteau |
| Poissonnerie: | la crevette | l'huître |
| Épicerie: | l'huile | le sel |

## 5.5

1. checkered 2. silk 3. loose 4. short 5. sleeve
6. cloth 7. scarf 8. slipper

## 5.6

1. raccommoder 2. repasser 3. laver 4. tailleur 5. retoucher

## 5.7

1. la montre 2. le bracelet 3. la broche 4. la poudre 5. la pince

## 5.8

1. f 2. h 3. g 4. a 5. d
6. e 7. c 8. b

## 5.9

1. a 2. f 3. e 4. h 5. c
6. b 7. d 8. g

## 5.10

1. W 2. MW 3. W 4. M 5. M
6. MW

## 5.11

| 1. V | 2. V | 3. V | 4. F | 5. V |
|------|------|------|------|------|

6. F

## 6.1

| 1. E | 2. D | 3. B | 4. C | 5. A |
|------|------|------|------|------|

## 6.2

1. les toilettes/les WC/les   2. la cuisine/kitchenette   3. le balcon/la
   cabinets/la salle de bains                                 terrasse

4. le salon/la salle de séjour   5. la chambre à coucher

## 6.3

| 1. immeuble | 2. grenier | 3. salon | 4. fenêtre | 5. toit |
|-------------|------------|----------|------------|---------|

6. clé

## 6.4

| 1. c | 2. b | 3. e | 4. d | 5. a |
|------|------|------|------|------|

## 6.5

1. Je sors les ordures tous les jours.
2. Anne allume la lumière sur la terrasse.
3. Nous avons un nouveau frigo.
4. La serviette est sale.
5. Je dois ranger ma chambre.
6. Nous ne lavons pas souvent les fenêtres du salon.
7. Tu fais la cuisine le week-end?
8. Il me faut un balai et une pelle.

## 6.6

| 1. F | 2. F | 3. V | 4. F | 5. F |
|------|------|------|------|------|

| 6. V | 7. F | 8. F |
|------|------|------|

## 6.7

1. sponge  2. spoon  3. cutlery  4. napkins  5. dustpan

6. tray

## 6.8

Answers will vary.

## 7.1

1. V  2. F  3. V  4. F  5. V

6. V  7. F  8. V  9. F  10. V

## 7.2

1. c  2. d  3. e  4. b  5. a

## 7.3

1. c  2. a  3. e  4. b  5. d

## 7.4

1. raise  2. salary  3. sick leave  4. mortgage  5. job

6. strike  7. vacancy  8. retirement  9. union  10. take a long weekend

## 7.5

1. économiser  2. épargne  3. versement  4. intérêts  5. prêt

6. actions  7. en hausse  8. dettes

## 7.6

1. accumuler  2. relevé  3. échanger  4. branche  5. prêt

6. coffre-fort  7. retirer  8. fonds

## 7.7

1. C      2. B      3. E      4. F      5. A

6. D      7. G      8. H

## 7.8

1. réserve      2. baissé      3. salaire      4. coût de la vie

5. faillite

## 8.1

1. f      2. c      3. e      4. h      5. b

6. g      7. a      8. d

## 8.2

1. V      2. F      3. V      4. V      5. F

6. V      7. F      8. F

## 8.3

1. c      2. b      3. a      4. c      5. d

6. d      7. b      8. a      9. b      10. d

## 8.4

1. Noël/Veille de Noël      2. Nouvel An/Saint-Sylvestre      3. Jour du Poisson/premier avril

4. Veille de Noël ou du Nouvel An      5. Fête Nationale      6. Saint-Valentin

7. Anniversaire de mariage      8. Carnaval

## 8.5

1. la disco (discothèque)      2. le cinéma      3. le musée/la galerie d'art

4. la patinoire      5. la Fête du livre/la librairie

**8.6**

| 1. c | 2. e | 3. a | 4. f | 5. h |
|------|------|------|------|------|
| 6. g | 7. b | 8. d | | |

**8.7**

| 1. A | 2. F | 3. E | 4. C | 5. D |
|------|------|------|------|------|
| 6. H | 7. G | 8. B | 9. J | 10. I |

**8.8**

1. J'adore aller à la plage et nager dans l'océan.
2. Le camping est amusant.
3. Tu joues aux dames?/Tu joues au jeu de dames?
4. Il collectionne les vieilles voitures.
5. J'aime bien bavarder avec mes amis sur Internet.
6. Je lis des livres de science-fiction.
7. Zut alors! J'ai effacé un e-mail.
8. Je fais du jogging dans le parc près de chez moi.
9. Mon équipe favorite ne gagne pas toujours.
10. Les mots croisés sont quelquefois difficiles.

**8.9**

| 1. F | 2. F | 3. V | 4. V | 5. V |
|------|------|------|------|------|
| 6. F | 7. V | 8. V | | |

**8.10**

| 1. le gant | 2. la piscine | 3. l'épée | 4. la piste |
|------------|---------------|-----------|-------------|
| 5. le gardien de but | 6. le vélo | | |

**8.11**

Answers will vary.

**9.1**

| 1. 5 | 2. 4 | 3. 1 | 4. 2 | 5. 3 |
|------|------|------|------|------|

## 9.2

| 1. f | 2. d | 3. g | 4. a | 5. h |
|---|---|---|---|---|
| 6. c | 7. e | 8. b | | |

## 9.3

| 1. F | 2. F | 3. V | 4. F | 5. F |
|---|---|---|---|---|
| 6. V | 7. V | 8. F | | |

## 9.4

| 1. brochures | 2. forfait | 3. syndicat | 4. agence | 5. périmé |
|---|---|---|---|---|
| 6. change | 7. hors-taxe | 8. vacances | | |

## 9.5

| 1. overbooking | 2. landing | 3. stopover | 4. headset |
|---|---|---|---|
| 5. commuter pass | 6. platform/dock | 7. bus station/ train station | 8. life buoy |
| 9. tide | 10. ocean liner | | |

## 9.6

| 1. d | 2. a | 3. b | 4. e | 5. c |
|---|---|---|---|---|

## 9.7

| 1. d | 2. a | 3. c | 4. e | 5. b |
|---|---|---|---|---|
| 6. g | 7. h | 8. f | | |

## 10.1

| 1. V | 2. F | 3. F | 4. V | 5. F |
|---|---|---|---|---|
| 6. V | 7. V | 8. F | 9. V | 10. V |

## 10.2

| 1. président | 2. cabinet | 3. secrétaire | 4. roi | 5. cinq |
|---|---|---|---|---|

## 10.3

1. d          2. a          3. b          4. c          5. d

## 10.4

1. boycott    2. compromis  3. salariés   4. médiateurs 5. syndicat

## 10.5

1. 5          2. 10         3. 1          4. 7          5. 2
6. 9          7. 6          8. 8          9. 3          10. 4

## 10.6

1. puissance  2. sanctions  3. paix       4. accord     5. guerre
6. métier     7. victimes   8. otages     9. piégée     10. militaire

## 10.7

1. La diplomatie est la meilleure manière de préserver la paix.
2. La réunion au sommet a lieu à New York.
3. On va signer un traité de paix bientôt.
4. Dans chaque guerre il y a des objecteurs de conscience.
5. La défaite est toujours humiliante.
6. Les hostilités continuent.
7. Nous allons gagner la guerre.
8. On a déclaré un état d'urgence.
9. Le navire porte-avions est dans le golfe.
10. On vient d'attraper un espion.

## 11.1

1. étoiles    2. lune       3. galaxies   4. grottes
5. montagnes  6. ruisseaux  7. l'embouchure
8. étangs     9. nord       10. occidentale

## 11.2

1. la foudre      2. le vent      3. orageux      4. le tonnerre

5. la latitude

## 11.3

| | | | | |
|---|---|---|---|---|
| 1. V | 2. F | 3. V | 4. V | 5. F |
| 6. V | 7. F | 8. F | 9. F | 10. V |

## 11.4

| | | | | |
|---|---|---|---|---|
| 1. c | 2. e | 3. d | 4. a | 5. b |

## 11.5

| | | | | |
|---|---|---|---|---|
| 1. f | 2. c | 3. e | 4. a | 5. d |
| 6. b | | | | |

## 11.6

| | | | | |
|---|---|---|---|---|
| 1. F | 2. V | 3. F | 4. F | 5. F |
| 6. V | 7. V | 8. V | 9. F | 10. V |

## 11.7

1. le chêne      2. la tulipe      3. le dindon      4. le lapin

5. l'autruche      6. le moufette

## 11.8

| | | | | |
|---|---|---|---|---|
| 1. D | 2. E | 3. A | 4. F | 5. C |
| 6. B | | | | |

## 11.9

| | | | | |
|---|---|---|---|---|
| 1. c | 2. i | 3. h | 4. f | 5. a |
| 6. e | 7. b | 8. d | 9. g | 10. j |

### 11.10

1. La côte est une région désertique.
2. Le docteur Ray étudie les volcans.
3. Nous avons besoin de plus de forêt vierge.
4. Cette région est montagneuse.
5. Elle a glissé jusqu'au bas de la pente.
6. La rivière inonde la vallée chaque printemps.
7. L'eau de l'étang est polluée.
8. Nous nageons en amont.
9. Les vagues sont hautes.
10. Prenons une photo de la cascade.

### 12.1

| 1. g | 2. d | 3. f | 4. h | 5. a |
| 6. b | 7. e | 8. c | | |

### 12.2

| 1. bouteille | 2. grammes | 3. douzaine | 4. soixantaine | 5. bouchée |
| 6. pincée | 7. tranches | 8. autant | | |

### 12.3

| 1. F | 2. V | 3. V | 4. F | 5. F |
| 6. V | | | | |

### 12.4

| 1. c | 2. b | 3. b | 4. a | 5. b |

### 12.5

| 1. e | 2. b | 3. a | 4. f | 5. d |
| 6. c | | | | |

## 12.6

| 1. h | 2. g | 3. b | 4. c | 5. i |
|------|------|------|------|------|
| 6. j | 7. a | 8. f | 9. d | 10. e |

## 12.7

1. C'est au premier étage.
2. Nous sommes le 4 juillet./Aujourd'hui c'est le 4 juillet.
3. Le dixième chapitre est amusant.
4. Le cinquième match était le meilleur.
5. J'aime le cheval dans la neuvième course.
6. Nous ne sommes plus au vingtième siècle.
7. C'est la deuxième semaine du mois.
8. Novembre est le onzième mois de l'année.